# The Entrepreneur's Internet Handbook

## Your Legal and Practical Guide to Starting a Business Website

SPHINX® PUBLISHING
AN IMPRINT OF SOURCEBOOKS, INC.®
NAPERVILLE, ILLINOIS
www.SphinxLegal.com

First Edition, 2003

Published by: **Sphinx® Publishing, An Imprint of Sourcebooks, Inc.®**

Naperville Office
P.O. Box 4410
Naperville, Illinois  60567-4410
630-961-3900
Fax: 630-961-2168
www.sourcebooks.com
www.SphinxLegal.com

This publication is designed to provide accurate and authoritative information in regard
to the subject matter covered. It is sold with the understanding that the publisher is not
engaged in rendering legal, accounting, or other professional service. If legal advice or
other expert assistance is required, the services of a competent professional person
should be sought.

*From a Declaration of Principles Jointly Adopted by a Committee of the*
*American Bar Association and a Committee of Publishers and Associations*

**Library of Congress Cataloging-in-Publication Data**
O'Neill, Julia K.
  The entrepreneur's internet handbook : your legal and practical guide
to starting a business website / by Julia K. O'Neill and Hugo Barreca.
    p.  cm.
  ISBN 1-57248-251-6  (pbk.)
 1.  Electronic commerce--Law and legislation--United States--Popular
works. 2.  Business law--United States. 3.  Electronic commerce--Popular
works.  I. Barreca, Hugo. II. Title.
KF390.B84 O54 2003
343.7309'944--dc21
                                                                          2002152740

Printed and bound in the United States of America.

VHG Paperback — 10  9  8  7  6  5  4  3  2  1

# CONTENTS

**Section Two: Financing Your Internet Business**

**Section Three: Setting Up Your Website**

# Introduction

The Internet has changed our world. Gathering information, buying goods and services, finding people, making travel reservations and more can now be done from the comfort of your own chair. Businesspeople need to be aware of the new ways consumers do business in order to compete in the new economy.

Whether you are starting a new business, or just getting around to putting your existing business on the World Wide Web, you will probably have many questions about how to legally and practically reach the consumers who use the Internet to buy or research goods and services, or even just to find a business's name, address and phone number.

This book will help you through issues surrounding what structure to use for your business; how to reserve your domain name; how to go about setting up a website; what should be on your website; legal issues of which you should be aware when setting up your website and doing business on the Web; and, more. Checklists, charts, and a glossary are also provided for quick reference.

From the one-page site providing contact information to the complex shopping site, this book will guide you through the legal and practical issues you need to consider when you put your business on the Web. Have fun becoming cyber-savvy!

# SECTION I

## Setting-Up and Maintaining Your Business

# Chapter 1
## Choosing a Form of Entity

## The Right Entity for the Original Company

One of the first decisions any entrepreneur must make is the choice of entity for a new business. Should it be a corporation, partnership, limited partnership, limited liability company (LLC), or sole proprietorship?

There are also limited liability partnerships, limited liability limited partnerships, and professional corporations. Professionals such as architects and doctors are restricted by state laws to certain types of entities for practicing their professions. They are usually the only ones to use these last three types of entities.

### Limited Liability

The major benefit to forming a *corporation* or a *limited liability company* (LLC), rather than operating through a *partnership* or a *sole proprietorship*, is "limited liability." That is, if you properly create and maintain a corporation or an LLC to house your business, your personal assets (and your co-owners' personal assets) will not be subject to claims against the company.

Let us say you start a dog grooming business. You do not use a corporation, but operate as a sole proprietorship, which is not a limited liability entity. A dog attacks a visitor. The visitor sues you. Whether or not you are found liable for the injury, if your business is a sole proprietorship, you may have to exhaust your personal assets (including selling your house), to either pay to defend yourself in the lawsuit or to satisfy a judgment if you default (fail to defend yourself). If the business was operated as a corporation, you may have to exhaust the business's assets to pay for the suit, and perhaps even close up shop.

Once you put your business out on the Internet, you reach all kinds of people, all over the place. They will be reading your information, perhaps buying things from you, and whatever else your website attempts to entice them to do. The mere fact that you are now exposing your business to the whole world is a good reason to conduct your business through a limited liability entity.

So, assuming you want to do business through a limited liability entity, the next issue is to decide which one. The three most common entities used are the *C corporation*, the *S corporation*, and the *LLC*. Limited partnerships are also still in use, but they do not limit the personal liability of the general partner. If the general partner is a corporation or an LLC, this will not be a concern. Sole proprietorships and partnerships do not limit the liability of the owners—their assets are subject to the liabilities of the entity.

There is no legal requirement that one *must* use an attorney to form a company. You can just make a decision and file. That said, there are pros and cons for each type of entity. The answer can be different for each person's circumstances, so it is not easy to provide a formulaic answer.

## The Corporation

A corporation is an artificial, legal "person." That is, a corporation is treated as an independent entity with its own legal identity that allows it to carry on business and also subjects it to legal claims and obligations. The officers and directors of a corporation run its business for the ultimate benefit of its shareholders. In many states, one person may form a corporation and be the sole shareholder and officer.

Each state has its own set of laws governing corporations, including how they must be organized, how they must be governed, how often they must hold shareholders' meetings, how they can be merged or consolidated, how they can be dissolved, and various other matters. In general, the shareholders elect the directors, and the directors elect the officers. The officers have authority to run the day-to-day operations, but they need directors' approval to do anything out of the ordinary, such as sign a lease for business space, hire an executive employee, or start a new line of business. For even more major decisions such as sale of all of the assets of the corporation, merger, reorganization, consolidation, or amendment to the *certificate of incorporation* (in some states, this is called the *articles of organization*), a shareholders' vote is required.

An amendment to the certificate of incorporation is required in order to increase the number of authorized shares of stock, add another class or series of stock, change the corporation's name (although sometimes a shareholders' vote is not required to do this) and to take various other actions. In most states a majority shareholder vote is required to take most actions which require a shareholder vote, but for certain matters in certain states a two-thirds vote or other vote is required.

## The S Corporation

An S corporation is a corporation that has filed IRS Form 2553, choosing to have all profits taxed to the shareholders rather than to the corporation. Not all corporations are eligible for S corporation status. The S corporation can have no more than 75 shareholders. These shareholders must be individuals or certain types of trusts, estates or tax-exempt organizations. The company may only have one class of stock, or more than one class if the only differences are voting differences. All shareholders must be "natural" persons (this means an actual human being, rather than a legal "person" like a corporation). They cannot be non-resident aliens.

An S corporation files a corporate tax return, but pays no federal tax. The profit shown on the S corporation's tax return is reported on the owners' tax returns. In some states, even an S corporation must pay a corporate excise tax.

If an entity begins as an S corporation, but then violates one of the criteria required to remain an S corporation, it converts automatically by operation of law to a C corporation. No filing is required. A corporation can also voluntarily elect to terminate its S corporation status.

## The C Corporation

A C corporation is any business corporation that has not elected to be taxed as an S corporation. A C corporation pays income tax on its profits, unlike an S corporation, which does not. If a profitable C corporation then pays dividends to its shareholders, the income is taxed an additional time at the shareholder level, thus taxing the same revenues twice.

## The Professional Corporation

A *professional corporation* is a corporation formed by a professional such as a doctor or an accountant. State laws have special rules for professional service corporations which differ slightly from those of other corporations. Professional corporations can be either C or S corporations.

State laws generally require each shareholder and certain of the officers and directors of a professional corporation to be a licensed practitioner of the profession that the corporation has been organized to practice. When filing the organizational documents, the incorporators of a professional corporation generally have to obtain proof from the appropriate licensing board that the necessary persons are duly licensed. In addition, state law generally prohibit the issuance or transfer of shares to a person who is not professionally licensed. The various licensing boards also often have authority, by statute, to promulgate additional requirements with which professional corporations must comply.

## The Nonprofit Corporation

A *nonprofit corporation* is usually used for such organizations as churches and condominium associations. However, with careful planning, some types of businesses can be structured as nonprofit corporations and save a fortune in taxes. While a nonprofit corporation cannot pay dividends, it can pay its officers, directors and other employees fair salaries that are competitive with those paid by for-profit corporations.

## Corporate Advantages

There are many advantages to doing business as a corporation. If a corporation is properly organized and maintained, shareholders have no liability for corporate debts and lawsuits, and officers and directors usually have no personal liability for their corporate acts. The existence of a corporation may be perpetual, unlike a sole proprietorship or partnership. There are also tax advantages allowed only to corporations. There may be prestige in owning a corporation; capital may be raised by issuing stock; and it is easy to transfer ownership upon death. A small corporation can be set up as an S corporation to avoid corporate taxes but still retain corporate advantages. Some types of businesses can be created as non-profit corporations that provide significant tax savings.

For example, in a corporation, not all amounts paid out to employees are subject to self-employment tax—only salaries are subject to this tax. Other amounts distributed, as dividends, for example, are not subject to self-employment tax (assuming the tax authorities do not exercise their right to re-characterize income). In a sole proprietorship, partnership or LLC, generally all amounts paid out to employees, whether salary or not, will be subject to self-employment tax.

## Corporate Disadvantages

There are also disadvantages to the corporate structure. There are start-up costs for forming a corporation, and there are certain formal actions that are required such as annual meetings, maintaining separate bank accounts and filing tax forms. Unless a corporation registers as an S corporation it must pay federal income tax separate from the tax paid by the owners, and may pay more than the minimum state income tax.

# The Limited Partnership

A limited partnership has characteristics similar to both a corporation and a partnership. There are two types of partners. *General partners* have the control and liability. *Limited partners* invest money and have liability limited to what they paid for their share of the partnership (like corporate stock).

The main advantage to a limited partnership over other types of entities is that limited partners who have no control of the business or liability for its debts can contribute capital. However, general partners are personally liable for partnership debts and for the acts of one another. There also may be high start-up costs because a written limited partnership agreement is required. These can be very complicated. If you are considering a limited partnership, contact an attorney to draft this type of agreement.

# The Limited Liability Company

The limited liability company is quickly gaining in popularity. This entity has characteristics of both a corporation and a partnership. None of the members has liability and all can have some control. The limited liability company offers the tax benefits of a partnership with the protection from liability of a corporation. It offers more tax benefits, in some cases, than an S corporation because it may pass through more depreciation and deductions. This type of corporation may have different classes of ownership, an unlimited number of members and may have noncitizens and legal entities such as trusts or corporations as members. It is also extremely flexible in structure and operational aspects. Tax attributes such as losses may be allocated among the members in a manner different than according to their respective ownership interests in the company, with certain restrictions.

There are start-up costs associated with forming a limited liability company. It is advisable to have an operating agreement, drafted by an attorney, which can be complex and expensive. However, in many cases the benefits of an LLC will far outweigh the costs.

# The Choice between S Corporation and LLC

Often the entrepreneur will narrow the choice down to S corporation vs. LLC. Don't let yourself be talked into forming an LLC just because your attorney or advisor thinks it is the "trendy" thing to do. An S corporation can be a much simpler, cheaper entity to form, and in many instances can fill the same needs as an LLC with much less cost and complication. If your entity is eligible for S corporation status, ask yourself if it is really preferable to choose an LLC rather than an S corporation.

Tax issues may determine the final decision between the two entities. One tax aspect to consider is that *all income* of an LLC will be subject to self-employment tax. This is separate and in addition to income tax. With an S corporation, only salaries are subject to self-employment tax. If S corporation shareholders receive dividends as well as salaries, the dividends will not be subject to self-employment tax. (Note in this regard that the IRS has broad authority to re-characterize income as it sees fit.)

There is a second tax difference between the two entities that has to do with *distributions of property* (not salaries or cash dividends but assets owned by the company) that has increased in value since it went into the company. Distributions of such property out of an LLC to its members will generally be tax-free. The members will have a *carry over basis* in the distributed assets.

The *basis* of property is generally the purchase price. Basis is used, among other things, to determine gain or loss upon the sale or other disposition of property. If a taxpayer has a "carryover basis" in property transferred to him from another taxpayer, this means he can treat the transferor's cost as his own cost, for tax purposes (rather than having to use the current fair market value of the property as his basis).

As an example, assume an LLC buys a painting for $100. Several years later, the painting is worth $1000, and the LLC transfers it to one of its members. The member will not have any taxable event because of the transfer, and he will take the LLC's basis of $100 as his own basis—if he sells later for $2000, his gain will be the difference between the sale price ($2000) and his basis ($100). If the same transaction occurred between an S-corporation and a shareholder, the shareholder would have to take the current fair market value at the time of transfer of the painting ($1000) as his basis, and he would also have taxable gain at that time in the amount of the current value of the painting ($1000) minus the corporation's basis ($100).

Talk to your accountant if you think this could possibly happen with your business. With an S corporation, distributed appreciated assets will cause shareholders to have taxable income. Their basis is current fair market value in the assets. This is the major reason conversion from an S corporation to an LLC creates tax issues, while conversion from an LLC to an S corporation generally does not.

A third tax difference is that in the LLC, as stated earlier, owners can have allocations of tax benefits, such as depreciation and losses, that are different than their pro rata ownership interests. The S corporation cannot make special allocations of these tax items. The allocations are in direct proportion to the percentage of shares held by each individual.

Some tax issues vary state by state. For example, there is a major tax problem for a Massachusetts LLC engaged in a business that carries inventory. The personal property tax statutes specifically exempt personal property of a domestic business corporations, but not of an LLC. This means that an LLC with substantial personal property (i.e., inventory such as automobiles) will be liable for property tax. A Sub-s corporation would not owe any taxes. This legislative omission could be a costly trap for some businesses.

Plenty of people make decisions about choice of entity and file the necessary papers without the assistance of an attorney or accountant. Sometimes it works out, and sometimes it doesn't. You may save yourself some headaches by consulting with a professional at the outset. As noted above, state laws differ in their treatment of these different entities, especially the newer LLCs. Making the right choice in the beginning can save you lots of trouble, time, and money. It's harder to change the form of entity later, than it is to take the time and money to make the *right* choice now.

# Doing Deals through Partners, Subsidiaries, or Affiliates

When you are starting up your business, you may have a one-track business plan: make widgets and sell them on your website. You decide to form an S corporation to house your business.

After you've been doing business for a few months, you realize that many of your customers are requesting widgets with built-in modems. You have a friend who is good at modifying your widgets to include a built-in modem, and you think you can both make some money on this new project.

At this point, you need to consider whether your new line of business needs to be separated from your original line. You may want to keep the revenues from the two products completely separated. You may want to sell the new product under a different name. You may not want your friend to own any part of the business selling the first product. A major consideration should be whether the liabilities associated with the two different product lines should be segregated.

Does one product have greater inherent product liability risks? The company has a greater risk of being sued if its product is more dangerous. Will it be sold to a different type of market? Do you want the assets being generated by the first product line to be subject to liabilities generated by the second product line? Probably not. You will have to weigh against these issues the costs, in terms of money, time and hassles, of creating a separate legal entity for the new product line. It will almost always be worth it.

What should the relationship between the two entities be? Perhaps they will both be S corporations. You will be the sole owner of one, and you and your friend will be the co-owners of the other. The two corporations could enter into a contract providing for shared office space, shared website, and shared overhead costs. Or, maybe you and your friend decide that you will both own the original corporation, and you will create a new corporation, which will be owned by the first corporation (this is a subsidiary).

You may decide to just try things out temporarily with some type of *joint venture agreement* between your original corporation and your friend. A joint venture agreement is legally a partnership. Your friend may not have any assets to speak of, so he may not be concerned about liability issues. You also may not want to spend the resources to set up a new legal entity, when you do not know if the new venture will succeed.

In summary, there are many considerations in making the decision about the structure of a new business deal or venture. Tax issues, liability, ownership, length of the venture, physical location issues, and more will all need to be examined. Unfortunately, there is no simple formula for making the correct choice. However, if you know the basic differences among the different structures, you are well on your way to making the best decision for your business.

# Chapter 2

# Formation and Maintenance of Your New Entity

## Creating Structures that Anticipate Change

When you first set up your entity, try to leave room for new circumstances you do not currently anticipate. For example, if you think you will be the only owner of the business forever, don't make the mistake of authorizing only 100 shares when you create your corporation with the state, if the same filing fee can get you 200,000 authorized shares. You don't have to issue all 200,000—but at least there will be shares available down the line in the event you want to raise money through the sale of stock, issue stock to coworkers, etc. The state will always let you increase the number of authorized shares later, for a fee, but why pay for them, if you can get them up front for nothing?

You should also think about restrictions on transfer of your entity's shares or units. Let us say you are going into business with your best friend. You both plan to work at the business full-time. You form an S corporation and you each put in money and get 100 shares.

Now your best friend's wife gets an unbelievable job offer that she has been wanting for years. The job is in their hometown. Your best friend wants her to take the job, but it will mean they move 500 miles from where you are now living.

What happens to your friend's stock? Does he stop working with you, but still own 50% of the corporation and thus get an equal share of any dividends declared? You can put an agreement in place which will give the company, or you, or both, the option to buy a shareholder's shares if the shareholder stops working for the company, becomes disabled, or dies.

Do not wait until something happens to put this into place. Once you need it, it may be impossible to agree on the terms. Typically, this document is referred to as a *Shareholder's Agreement* or a *Buy-Sell Agreement.* It provides a way to create an agreed-upon plan of action in anticipation of several possible eventualities.

An important consideration for the correct choice of structure is the exit strategy contemplated by the business owners. For example, if your idea is to eventually merge with another company or to go public in an *Initial Public Offering of Stock* (IPO), you might choose a structure such as a C corporation which allows a merger or IPO more readily than an LLC.

Additionally, as noted above in the section dealing with tax issues, conversion from an S corporation to an LLC creates tax issues, while conversion from an LLC to an S-corporation generally does not. While it is possible to start out with one type of entity and to change later, do not delay the effort to determine the right legal structure in the formation of your company. An investment of your time in this effort at the beginning of the enterprise could save you triple the effort to change the structure later.

## Limiting your Liabilities During (*and after*) the Life of Your Business

You may have heard of *piercing the corporate veil.* This is what a court can do if it thinks that the owners of a corporation should be held personally liable for the corporation's liabilities and obligations. The court may do this if it finds that the owners have misused the corporate entity in some way, or have failed to put the public on notice that their business is being done through a corporate entity.

# Avoiding the Piercing of Your Corporate Veil

First, make sure that you put the entity's actual legal name, including the "Inc.," "Corp.," "LLC," or whatever it is, on everything. This means, on contracts, stationery, business cards, and especially, your website. (This author comes across websites all the time that fail to alert the viewer that the business entity has limited liability.)

Some corporations call their owners *partners*. Legally, partners have unlimited personal liability, even for the acts of the other partners. Do not call yourselves partners unless that is your true legal status. A creditor can argue that because your website said you were "partners," he thought you were personally obligated to pay the bills. The judge may just agree with him. Even if you do not use the word "partners," simply omitting the use of the real legal name, which includes the "Inc." or the like, makes it look to the world like you are a partnership or sole proprietorship.

If you are one person in business, and you do not have limited liability, you are a sole proprietorship. If you are more than one person in business, and you do not have limited liability, you are by definition a partnership. It does not matter that you have no written or verbal partnership agreement, or that the business is not called a "partnership." That is what the law says you are, and that is what a judge or jury may say you are if you do not put the public on notice that you are a limited liability entity.

There are many factors that a court will consider in determining whether to pierce the veil. Following is a list of things you should note carefully in order to avoid placing your personal assets at risk:

- keep your entity's assets separate from other persons' and entities' assets;
- have adequate books and records;
- have sufficient assets to meet its reasonably foreseeable needs (this is known as being *adequately capitalized*);
- business and operations should be kept separate from other persons' and entities' businesses and operations;

- hold annual meetings, if required by law, and keep appropriate minutes of meetings;

- take formal votes, if required by law, for all major decisions, and keep written records of these votes;

- have required officials, such as officers and directors, who specifically function as required by law;

- do not allow the use of its assets for anyone's personal purposes;

- do not promise anyone that you will be personally liable for the business's obligations, unless required to complete a transaction (such as a personal guaranty of a bank loan);

- make appropriate tax and other governmental filings in a timely manner; and,

- always use the entity's true legal name, unless it has filed a *fictitious name certificate.*

A *fictitious name certificate* is a document that is filed with the government (town, city, county or state, depending on where you live) that puts the public on notice that you or your entity is doing business through a "trade name," or name other than its (or your) true legal name. For example, if you are a sole proprietor and you have set up shop as "Bill's Grills," you are legally required to file a fictitious name certificate with the appropriate governmental authority to let the public know who the actual business owner is. This is especially important for any limited liability entity doing business through any name other than its true legal name, as the failure to make this filing can lead to the piercing of the corporate veil.

If your business ceases operations, be sure to notify all parties with whom you have dealt. Put a sign up; put a notice on your website; and, send a form letter to everyone with whom you have done business. The most important thing is to make sure that persons and entities that do or have done business with you or your entity are clearly informed that they are not transacting business with you as an individual. If you cease to operate, spend the few hundred dollars it takes to dissolve your corporation or other entity. This will put the public on notice that the entity no longer exists and will protect you in the long run.

# Chapter 3
## Contract Basics

Almost everyone who is in any kind of business will have dealings with some type of contract at some point. This chapter is aiming to give you a basic understanding of contract law.

A *contract* is an agreement among two or more parties. In most cases, it can be verbal or written. Most states have specific laws regarding which types of contracts must be in writing to be enforceable. In most states, for example, contracts involving the sale of goods for $500 or more and contracts involving the purchase and sale of real estate must be in writing to be enforceable. There are specific state laws governing other aspects of certain types of contracts, as well. Most states have adopted the *Uniform Commercial Code*, which governs contracts for the sale of goods, among other things.

## Pros and Cons

There are advantages and disadvantages to putting a contract in writing, rather than just making a verbal contract. The primary advantage to a written contract is that if there ever is a dispute as to the terms or existence of the agreement, the written contract provides ready proof of what the arrangement actually is. It also may assist the parties involved, by forcing them to define or specify the various terms of the deal. Sometimes the parties may not even have considered a certain aspect of the deal, until they go to put everything down in writing.

However, this aspect of the written contract can also be a disadvantage. It may be so difficult to put things into writing, or so difficult to agree on the written terms, that a verbal contract may be much easier, quicker and cheaper to make. But in our experience, in almost every case except for the smallest, fastest deal, the advantages of putting a contract in writing by far outweigh the disadvantages.

## Contract Requirements

In order for a contract to be enforceable (other than the requirement that it be in writing in certain cases), there are several elements that must exist. These are as follows:

*Capacity; Authority.* Both parties must have the legal capacity to contract. They must not be minors or be mentally incompetent. Corporations and other legal entities are generally presumed to have the capacity to contract. However, the specific officer of the entity who signs the contract must have authority to do so—whether because of the normal functions of his office, or because of specific authority granted by the appropriate person or group (e.g., the Board of Directors of a corporation). In some cases, even where the person was not duly authorized to sign the contract, the contract may still be enforceable.

*Consideration.* There must be "consideration" flowing from each party to the other. This means that each party must be giving something to the other. Consideration can consist of mutual promises, money or property. If you say to Joe, "When I sell my stock, I will give you half the proceeds," this is not an enforceable contract without more, because Joe has not made any promise to you nor given you any other consideration for your promise. *Consideration must flow both ways.*

*Offer and Acceptance.* There must be an "offer" and "acceptance." The parties must come to a mutual agreement about who is doing what. If you fax Joe a letter saying that you will paint his house for $3000, there is no contract until he agrees to the deal. If he faxes you a letter in return, saying you can paint the house but I will only pay you $2500—that is a new offer, not an acceptance of your offer. There would not be a contract in that case until you accept Joe's offer (whether verbally or in writing. Again, it is much easier to prove a written contract than a verbal one).

Additionally, a counteroffer, such as Joe's proposal to pay you $2500, serves immediately as a refusal of your original offer. Consequently, you are no longer bound to paint his house for $3000 even if he decides later to accept your original deal. The counteroffer has taken your original offer from the table. You are free to come up with another price and start the negotiation over again. (Of course, he may later decide that he does want you to paint the house for $3000— and if you agree at that point you will have a deal.)

*Legal Subject Matter.* The subject matter of the contract cannot be "against public policy." The courts will not enforce a contract for illegal activities or other matters that are considered against public policy. For example, if Joe says he will pay you $500 to steal some item from a store, the contract is unenforceable because stealing is illegal.

## What to Include in Your Contract

In a written contract, it is very important to be precise and thorough. The obligations of each party should be thoroughly spelled out and defined. Most contracts should cover the following:

- specific time frames for performance;

- specific time frames for payment;

- length of time the contract will be in effect (this is not always applicable – if the arrangement is for one isolated transaction, this provision may be omitted);

- form of payment;

- details of performance—what exactly is to be done, how exactly it is to be done, who is to do it (if you contract with a corporation for consulting services, for example, you may want to specify actual persons that are to do the work). Words and obligations must be precisely defined;

- who pays for cost of materials and other expenses; time frames for payment;

- whether either party can terminate the contract prior to full performance, and under what circumstances;

- what happens if the contract is terminated;

- what state's law applies;

- in what state legal action or arbitration must be commenced;

- arbitration provisions (these can help speed up and lower the cost of resolving disputes, but are not recommended in all cases);

- representations and warranties by each party;

- remedies (some matters lend themselves to the remedy of "specific performance"—this means that the court or arbitrator can force the breaching party to perform his obligations under the contract, rather than just pay damages to the non-breaching party);

- notice and cure provisions for breach (not always appropriate);

- specified damages to be paid in the event of breach (also not always appropriate or enforceable);

- whether the contract is *assignable* (that is, you or the other party can assign someone else to be responsible for performance called for in the contract);

- how to give notice to the other party and when notice is deemed given (e.g., on the date of mailing by first class mail or on the date of hand delivery); and,

- whether there are any other agreements that form a part of the deal.

Some contracts are perfectly understandable by the non-attorney, and you may feel comfortable entering into them without legal assistance. Sometimes if both parties have an attorney it can complicate matters rather than simplify them. If you are confident that you understand all the terms of a contract and are comfortable with them, and that the contract covers everything, it may be fine to enter into the contract without having an attorney review it. But if you are entering a new area or signing a complex contract, you may do yourself a favor by hiring an attorney.

# Chapter 4
## Dealing with Employees

If you're starting a business, you may at some point have employees. Even if you are the only person working at the business, you will probably technically be an "employee." You will probably draw a salary, which will be subject to withholding taxes and the like. It is best to have a payroll service handle these tax filings, because the filings can be very cumbersome. The service is usually fairly affordable.

You may wonder what else needs to be in place if you hire other people to work for your company. Issues about hiring and firing, employment agreements, and employee policies may arise. This chapter discusses some of the basics you should consider if you are going to have employees.

## Discrimination

There are many federal and state laws that affect employers. Various laws prohibit discrimination in the context of hiring and firing, compensation, promotion, recruitment, use of facilities, fringe benefits, and other aspects of employment. Following are some of the federal laws with which you may need to comply. If any of these apply to your business, you should investigate the details of how to comply. You can find helpful information regarding these laws at the website of the Equal Employment Opportunity Commission:

www.eeoc.gov

| Applies To | Law |
|---|---|
| All employers | *Equal Pay Act of 1963*<br><br>Prohibits sex-based wage discrimination for men and women performing substantially the same work in the same establishment. |
| Employers with 15 or more employees | *Title VII of the Civil Rights Act of 1964*<br><br>Prohibits employment discrimination based on race, color, religion, sex or national origin.<br><br>*Title I and Title V of the Americans with Disabilities Act of 1990 (ADA)*<br><br>Prohibits discrimination against qualified individuals with disabilities in the private sector and state and local governments. |
| Employers with 20 or more employees | *Age Discrimination in Employment Act of 1967 (ADEA)*<br><br>Prohibits discrimination based on age; protects those 40 and older. |

In many cases, if a certain law applies to your business, you are required to post notices at your workplace, advising employees of their rights. The EEOC website will help you find out about these requirements as well. You should also check on your state's website for information about state and local laws with which you may need to comply.

# Hiring and Firing

In general, an employer is allowed to hire and fire whomever he or she wishes, subject to the types of laws described earlier. If you have not made a specific agreement with someone as to their term of employment, you can generally terminate their employment at any time for any reason or for no reason. However, you should be aware that various state courts have over time whittled away at this rule. Be careful not to promise employment for any certain length of time, whether verbally or in writing (unless, of course, you intend to make a contract with the employee along those lines), and whether expressly or by implication.

At some point, employees may have to be fired. To avoid charges of discrimination, and to maintain good human resources practices, written records of employee performance should be kept. Annual or semi-annual performance reviews should be conducted with each employee, and written evaluations should be shared with the employee and kept on permanent file.

If you do have to fire someone, keep written records of the events leading up to the firing. Have a witness present at the exit interview. Be sure to keep the discussion non-personal, professional, and short.

# Employment Agreements

There is no requirement that an employee have an employment agreement. Contracts are often used with executive-type employees, and often because the employee insists on a contract. There are various reasons why an employee would want a contract—to obligate the employer to employ him for a specified length of time, to specify compensation and bonuses, and to specify fringe benefits are examples.

Employment contracts usually are very specific as to the circumstances under which an employee can be terminated and whether the employer has to give the employee advance notice of the problem and an opportunity to fix it. Often a contract will provide that the employer cannot terminate the employment before the end of the stated term, unless there is "cause." "Cause" should be carefully and specifically defined. Often the definition will include the employee's being indicted or convicted of a crime involving "moral turpitude," absence from employment without good reason for a certain length of time, willful failure to perform the duties of employment, and disability. Entering into an employment contract is a serious matter, and you should seek legal counsel before doing so.

A major issue in many Internet-based business employee contracts is a covenant concerning competition with the signing company after the employee leaves the company. On one hand, the signing company does not want the employee to divulge any proprietary techniques to the next employer, and consequently wants to have a strong "non-compete" provision in the contract. On the other hand, the employee wants to be free to work anywhere and to use his or her full skill set at future positions.

In practice, *non-compete provisions* are usually a compromise between these two extremes. A non-compete that is too strict will not be enforced by the courts. It is a matter of public policy that people should be allowed to earn a living. Reasonable restrictions on employee competition will be enforced.

Reasonable non-competition clauses include an expiration date on the non-compete (6 months to two years are typical time frames) and cannot prevent the employee from using a generic skill set to work in the industry. For example, a programmer cannot be forced to abandon working as a programmer, even if she will be working for your competitor. She can be stopped from using proprietary programming techniques that have been invented or perfected at your company. She can also be restrained from soliciting other employees from your company to work for her new employer.

## Internet-Use and Email Policies

These days, especially since employees often have access to the Internet, it is important to put written policies in place as to what your employees are allowed to do at the workplace and/or using the employer's facilities and equipment. In addition to a stated Internet-use policy, filtering and monitoring software may help a business maintain its Internet use goals.

To formulate an Internet-use policy, you will have to examine your business's goals and objectives. The Internet can be used for many different business purposes—from financial, marketing, purchasing and shipping to training and project collaboration. Your business's Internet-use policy should encourage positive and constructive use of the Internet, as well as prevent or minimize use of the Internet for personal or inappropriate reasons. Your policy might prohibit employees from visiting adult sites, participating in chat rooms, shopping for non-business purposes, making personal travel plans, or any other non-work-related activity. Or, you could limit them to a certain amount of time per day for personal use of the Internet with your equipment.

Once you have your policy in place, consider using Internet-use software that can monitor your employees' use of the Internet, categorize the sites they visit, and keep track of the number of visits and the time spent there. The software can be used to generate reports that will tell you which employees are adhering to your policy and which are not. These reports may also help you to improve and tailor your policy. You should let your employees know that the software is being used. They should know that they have no expectation of privacy with regard to their Internet-use. Just knowing the software is in place may cause them to adhere to your policy.

In addition to monitoring software, you may want to put filtering software in place. You can use filters to completely block your employees' access to specified sites or types of sites (adult sites, for example).

You should also have a policy regarding email. You may want to restrict company email to company business—if so, you need to let your employees know that. They should also know that they have no expectation of privacy with regard to their work email account. If the system has a problem, some technical person may see all of your employees' emails. They should keep the personal information to a minimum for their own benefit.

Policy should also be made concerning "instant messenger-ing," or "I-M-ing" (pronounced "eye-emming"). Instant messages are those that pop up on a recipient's screen immediately after being typed and sent by the writer. If both people—or whole groups of people—are all logged onto the same I-M account, they can send messages back and forth among the whole group. It has not been unheard of for dozens of employees, who may even sit in the same room, to I-M each other for hours at a time, often joined by friends from outside the company who may also log on to the account. The use of this feature can get totally out of hand.

The Internet, when used appropriately, can help your business prosper. Misuse, however, can cause lack of productivity, interpersonal issues (if an employee sees personal information about another employee in an email, for example), and worse. Be educated and diligent in making the Internet work for you.

# SECTION 2
## FINANCING YOUR INTERNET BUSINESS

# Chapter 5
## FINANCING OPTIONS

This book is not designed to be a guide on the financial and legal details of raising money. There are many sources that can be used that are devoted exclusively to these subjects. Many professionals would be glad to help you through the process for a fee. However, in our experience, Internet businesses often need financing, either as a startup or an expansion of an already existing business. We therefore include this survey of topics that will familiarize you with the broad outlines of the financing landscape, focusing on subjects most closely related to the Internet entrepreneurial arena.

Depending on your circumstances, you may need to evaluate several options for financing your Internet business. You may be a start-up with no assets but a great idea or a proven management team. Or, you may already have an existing business that can provide funding for your new enterprise. You might have an existing business, but feel that new sources of funding would be a better choice for your start-up. You may be in excellent personal economic condition, but want to raise money in order to leave your other assets intact and to spread the risk. You may even have an Internet-based business on which a parallel venture could be built.

Each of these scenarios (and many others you can think of) presents its own set of strengths and weaknesses to the financing process. Each one has a blend of the three major elements that investors look for in deciding on investment opportunities.

# What Investors Invest In

In our experience, investors are willing to invest in three basic things: management, assets, or cash flow. In any money-raising endeavor, the entrepreneur must be prepared to meet all three of these investors, and may meet all three in the same room, each posing questions in their own ways. Of course, everyone's business is unique and you may touch on each of these issues in your own special way. Before meeting with potential investors, however, you should have in mind which ways your business is going to meet the demands posed by each of the following three considerations.

## Management

The investors are willing to entrust their money to a certain person or group of persons. The investors have faith that this management team will produce profits and cash. Management may have certain credentials or expertise that lends viability to a company. The management may simply have established an excellent track record with previous companies.

Some investors are willing to bet on certain managers regardless of the enterprise those managers have become involved in. Other investors see some unique characteristics in the management team that make them a good gamble. For example, they might be the inventors of a new process, or have important relationships in a certain industry or government sector. The investors are investing in the team.

Internet businesses are often started by dynamic management teams or by creative individuals who are enthusiastic about their concepts. Investors certainly want to see a zealous, if not evangelical, founder, but that is not enough, by itself, to get the funding you need. Make sure your management team demonstrates competence in key business areas such as marketing, sales, finance, and human resources. It should have the technical expertise to create and manage an Internet environment.

## Assets

Investors will invest in a physical device that does something or produces something new or better than existing devices. They will invest in a unique process that produces something or in intellectual property such as a patent or a trademark, or in software that produces a certain result. They may also invest in property, inventory, or other tangible goods.

This does not mean the investors don't care about management— they do. But in this case, investors may see management as stewards whose job is to manage the asset base. If the managers do a poor job, they might be replaced, leaving the asset base to be managed by another team. If needed, the asset can be sold or licensed.

Internet businesses don't necessarily have a lot of assets. Unfortunately, recent experience has demonstrated that Internet software costing millions of dollars cannot be resold at even a small fraction of its original cost, if the underlying business model fails. Additionally, computer hardware is not a very bankable asset because it rapidly depreciates in value. A useful life of three years is typical before computers become obsolete compared to newer models.

Internet-related businesses may be driven by patented software or be based on a unique process or methodology, but it is often difficult to provide a good valuation of this type of intellectual property. You may have to work hard to demonstrate how and why your assets should be valuable to a potential investor.

## Cash flow

Think of this investor as someone who sees a field as something to be mowed. This investor puts money into a business process that will reap the growth of this field. He or she looks for a circumstance and set of events that will produce *reliable cash flow*. (An example of reliable cash flow for an Internet business would be subscription revenue that is paid for use of a certain website.) Assets and management may be the key to making this happen, but this investor searches for opportunities in supply, demand, and marketing.

# Equity vs. Loans

## Equity investments

Someone who invests in your company by buying shares of stock, or a percentage of a limited liability company, is investing in the company itself. This is an *equity investment*. The investor hopes to receive cash at some time in the future, but that date and the amount of cash are uncertain at the time of the investment. The investors will own a part of your company and they will retain certain rights of ownership. Depending on the kind of stock or equity interest they receive, they may vote on decisions and attend meetings.

Some investors might be granted *preferred shares* or *equity interests* that command more executive powers. For example, preferred shareholders may have more voting power, or the only voting power, in the company. Preferred shareholders may also have the right to be first in line to be paid if the company declares dividends or is liquidated in case of failure.

Some investors may demand a seat on the Board of Directors or as a manager of a limited liability company. The investment may be made through a contract that provides them with additional powers, such as the right to approve expenditures over a certain dollar amount or to approve the start of a new line of business. However, the investors will pretty much sink or swim with you. They make money if you make money and they fail if you fail.

The cash that investors hope to receive may come in a variety of ways. Quite often, they hope the stock or other equity ownership of the company is purchased by another company in a merger, or by the public in an *Initial Public Offering*, or *IPO*. It is true that most often founders' stock or original investors' stock is not bought in an IPO, because such stock will be subject to restrictions on sale by the IPO underwriters.

No one wants to see managers and investors selling out of the company the day after the company is made public. However, this "lockup" of stock usually expires after six months or some other designated time period, after which the investors can put their shares on the market.

This receipt of cash in exchange for investments is referred to by a number of names, such as *Exit Strategy* or *Liquidity Event*. These expressions boil down to one thing—getting investments out of the company in cash. When approaching investors, it is paramount that you can demonstrate how and when they might be able to realize the value of their ownership in cash. Investors will want to know how they are going to recover their investments, and how long it will take to get there. While you should not guarantee future results, you do need to demonstrate how you think this will be achieved. Be specific—vague hopes for future fortune will not be acceptable.

## Loans

Loans are cash that must be paid back to the lender at some date and time certain, in amounts predetermined in the loan documents. Loans may be *secured* or *unsecured*. Secured loans are backed by collateral, which are assets of some kind that the lender will obtain in case you fail to pay back the loan. Unsecured loans are not backed by collateral and are much riskier for the lender. Unsecured loans usually command a higher interest rate to compensate the lender for taking the risk.

Lenders may insist that certain performance milestones be reached before funding is released. For example, a million dollar loan may start out with the disbursement of $100,000. When the company reaches certain milestones, such as a certain revenue target, the next amount of money will be disbursed. Lenders also often demand that the company maintain performance milestones by building in certain "covenants" that outline financial guidelines that the company must maintain in order to keep the loan active.

An example of this might be the average number of days it takes to collect money. If receivables on average age over 60 days, for example, the lender may not release more cash and may even demand the loan be repaid immediately. These performance covenants are not dictated by legal standards. They will be as easy or as difficult to comply with as you can manage to negotiate with the lender. Make sure you go over them carefully before borrowing money. Be aggressive in getting the best terms you can.

If for some reason you fail to repay the loan on time, the lender may be entitled to seize the assets you pledged as collateral. This may be the ownership of a portion of the company itself, or it might be other assets that have been pledged, including personal assets. Again, this is negotiable, and it is worth your time to know exactly what the terms are in order to get the absolute best terms you can manage under the circumstances.

## Convertible Notes

An instrument called a *convertible note* is a variation on an ordinary loan. It allows the lender the option of converting all or a part of the loan to equity, based on certain formulas. For example, someone might lend your company $50,000, with a payment of $1,000 plus interest due every month for fifty months, starting six months after the loan is disbursed. This loan is convertible to the company's stock at the rate of one dollar per share—meaning that the lender could decide to forgo receiving cash payment for the loan and receive stock instead.

This type of loan is desirable to both parties under certain conditions. The lender may be skeptical that your company's stock is ever going to be worth much, and so the lender prefers to get his money back in cash. But in the happy event that the lender is wrong, and your company's stock becomes valuable, or its prospects are looking good, the lender can convert whatever remains on the loan to the equivalent dollar amount in shares at the price agreed to in the loan documents.

For example, if the lender has received $20,000 back in cash, he could still choose to receive 30,000 shares of stock instead of taking the remainder of the loan in cash (ignore interest for this example). The borrower, especially a startup company strapped for cash, might be glad to trade shares in exchange for the loan to be removed from the company's obligations. The lender gets equity in the company at the point where he feels the company is worth the risk.

# Chapter 6
## Business Plans

Before considering any investments, investors and lenders will want to examine your plans for starting or expanding a business. This calls for a *business plan* to written. A written plan demonstrates that you have thought through all aspects of the challenges the business will face and lets potential investors review and discuss those items. It also allows you to capture ideas from various readers who may provide valuable insights on tactics and strategy. Equally important, it can serve as an internal tool for planning the future of the company and for making changes to the plan as the business develops.

## Nondisclosure Agreements

Written plans can be shared among an investor's colleagues. This is good in that you may interest investors beyond those with whom you've had personal contact. It is also *not* good in that others may appropriate your ideas before you get a chance to start-up your own enterprise. Therefore, it is wise to consider having all evaluators of your plan sign a nondisclosure agreement, often referred to as an "NDA." An *NDA* stipulates that the readers of the materials will not share the information with anyone else unless you approve it and that the reader acknowledges the ideas are proprietary.

Some investment companies will not sign NDA's as a matter of policy. This is because they may receive dozens or even hundreds of business plans each week. If they signed NDA's for each one, it would be a burdensome legal chore. Additionally, from a practical standpoint, they could never retain all the details of each NDA every time they picked up a plan. Finally, there is a potential for conflict in promising not to disclose almost everything they read without permission of the writer.

You must make up your mind whether or not to provide plans to those who will not sign an NDA. In our experience, investment bankers don't intend to steal anyone's business plans. It would be disastrous for their reputations if they did so. They are not in business as investment bankers in order to start-up a new company. Still, this has to be a judgment call on your part. You should research the firms before handing materials over to make sure they are legitimate investors or investment brokers.

## Sample Nondisclosure Agreements

Nondisclosure agreements can run to several pages and outline exactly when the reader can disclose the information. But even a simple one can serve to protect your interests. Something such as the following NDA should be on your plan at a minimum.

---

### Confidentiality Agreement

The undersigned reader acknowledges that the information provided by Company XYZ in this business plan is confidential; therefore, reader agrees not to disclose it without the express written permission of Company XYZ.

It is acknowledged by reader that information to be furnished in this business plan is in all respects confidential in nature, other than information which is in the public domain through other means, and that any disclosure or use of same by reader may cause serious harm or damage to Company XYZ.

*(continued)*

---

Upon request, this document is to be immediately returned to Company XYZ.

_____   _____

Signature                                    Date

_____

Name (typed or printed)

*This is a business plan.*
*It does not imply an offering of securities.*

## The Right Type of Business Plan for Your Needs

You should try to fit the scope and detail of your plan to fit the size and type of investment you seek.

A going concern that has a positive cash flow and a good track record might get a loan from a bank with a set of financial statements and a brief outline of the new enterprise—a total of ten to fifteen pages. An entrepreneur with a history of successes might need no more than that if he or she is approaching previous investors or those who know of his or her reputation. A start-up business with no operating history may not need much more than that, particularly if the investment being sought is relatively modest (in the hundreds of thousands). There is nothing to report about the past, and projections into the future are speculative at best.

More detailed plans are called for when the amount of investment being sought gets larger. A five million dollar target will certainly require detailed plans about operations, management history, workflow organization and detailed, multi-year financial projections.

It is much better to decide on the amount of money being sought and to fit the plan to the target than to simply start writing a plan and hope it all works out. Create an outline and delegate responsibilities if there is a team available to work on the project.

# Business Plan Contents

Good business plans contain certain key elements. They also contain the personal voice of the founder or founders. Professional business plan writers can be hired to help with this task; however, if you do take that route, make sure your voice comes through the rhetoric.

## The Executive Summary

As noted above, some investment professionals receive dozens or hundreds of plans every week. They need to sort through these quickly, sometimes to see if your proposed business fits their investment profile, and sometimes to allocate the plan to certain areas within the organization. For example, an Internet group may be designated to review those types of plans, versus other industry segments.

The *Executive Summary* needs to get the salient ideas into one or two pages. This is sometimes the hardest thing to do in the entire process. Some founders find it almost impossible to summarize their plans into succinct business terms. If you are having difficulty, seek advice and help from someone outside your group. This outside advisor might be able to provide the perspective needed to summarize your plans. (Note: It is not a legitimate option to squeeze five pages of summary into two pages by reducing the type face, expanding the margins, or other tricks. These plans often get into the trash pile within ten seconds of being opened.)

The executive summary should make clear:

- what your product, process or service is;
- your target market and the market's key characteristics;
- the strategy behind the plan;
- brief description of the management team and why they are suited to the plan (list past successes);
- amount of money being sought;
- how the money will be used;
- how the investors will get their investment back; and,
- a brief financial history, if appropriate.

Granted, this is a lot of information for a brief summary. It may be helpful to write the summary last, after all other elements are in the plan.

## Objectives

This should describe how your process, service, or product would distinguish itself in the marketplace. Make clear what it is and how it works. You must explain the value you bring to the market compared with your competition.

Your objectives should be both short term and long term. Avoid generalizations. A short-term objective might be "to generate $100,000 in revenue within six months," not "increase sales." Measurable goals are better than lofty aspirations. A long-term objective of "capturing 50 percent of the Internet health care market" is better than "improve the life of all Americans through better health care information."

## Your Company

Tell what type of entity the company is (corporation, LLC, etc.), where it is located, and who the owners are (so far). Provide its history, its current status, and its plans for the future. History can include motivations for starting the company if the company is recently formed. The current status should include a description of any divisions within the company (different lines of business, different markets, etc.) and company affiliates (subsidiaries, joint ventures, etc.).

## Market Analysis

Describe the target market and its size. Tell how long it has been identified as a market and what trends exist concerning that market. Describe what you see as its future prospects.

You should also describe how your product or service would benefit that marketplace better than existing competition; what the barriers are to enter the marketplace; and, how those barriers are seen by the competition. You must also describe how that marketplace will evolve in the future.

For example, a few years ago, Internet sites that focused on health-related issues had a huge marketplace—health care is a growing part of the world's economy. However, dozens of sites opened up to serve that market; only a few are left standing. If you are approaching the health-care market using an Internet presence, you need to describe how your services are going to distinguish themselves from existing survivors. You should also describe why you will not repeat the fates of those who closed up before you arrived. Another issue you need to explain is how your services won't be copied by existing health sites or potentially by newly established sites. Also discuss how trends in this marketplace are likely to affect your business.

## Market Segmentation

This is an important analysis, but sometimes not a well-understood aspect of the marketing component. This explains the salient behaviors within the market you are targeting. For example, in the health-related services described above, economic data may show that the bulk of the money is being spent by aging baby-boomers, who are making up a larger part of the health care economy. But look a little deeper, and data will show that aging baby-boomers may not use the Internet to research health issues as much as young adults. If you are targeting the baby-boomer market, you need to describe how you will address this particular issue.

## Management Team

A set of brief biographies here is better than full-blown résumés of every team member. You cannot expect investors to plow through everyone's individual life story, no matter how interesting. Be sure to present summarized important accomplishments of each individual on the management team, particularly those elements that will contribute to your plan's success. An appendix can contain the full résumés of all parties concerned, so the investors can review them in detail if desired.

## Strategy and Implementation Summary

This section should describe how you are going to execute your plan. It should explain research and development issues, manufacturing or distribution methods, quality controls, and any product regulation issues. It should describe how your organization would be structured to meet the demands of the business. It should cover stages of growth and be tied into the need and timing for cash during each phase. It should also describe the existence of any intellectual property and what protections are in place concerning that property.

## Sales and Marketing

This section should cover how your sales efforts will be organized and executed. It should also tell of the plans for marketing—how, to which groups, how frequently, on what media. Sales milestones are often presented at this juncture. Good ideas and good products don't sell themselves. Many analysts consider most businesses' success or failure to be tied directly to their marketing strategies (or lack thereof).

## Financial Forecasts

These should include:

- *Profit and loss statements.* Sales minus expenses = profit. (Many investors want to stop here, but the financial picture is not complete without the following two items.)

- *Cash flow statements.* This should include timing and amounts of investments required.

- *Balance sheet.* A list of assets and liabilities of the company at a particular moment in time, usually at the end of a financial reporting period (such as end-of-quarter or end-of-year).

# Dog and Pony Shows

Finally, you may have to present your plan to potential investors in what are called "dog and pony" shows. This is nothing more than an in-person presentation of your plan to potential investors. You might be asked to put together a slide-show or Power Point presentation of your plan so that the meeting moves along quickly.

A rule of thumb for presentations: no more than one heading and three bullet point items per slide. Most audiences dismiss crowded slides within seconds of their being put on the screen. Avoid the temptation to put cute icons or animated figures in the presentation. Keep the tone professional.

# Chapter 7
## Raising Equity

## Securities Registration

More than seventy years ago, federal legislation was enacted that put certain controls into place in the securities markets. Every state has also put similar controls into its statutes. Among the goals of these laws was the prevention of the kind of stock market crash that occurred in 1929 and the protection of investors. The laws require, among other things, that specific disclosures must be made to potential investors when selling securities, including audited financial statements and the filing of complex forms with the Securities and Exchange Commission ("SEC"), which, after approval (which may take months), allow you to "register" your securities with the SEC.

Securities registration is a complex process which may take hundreds of hours of professional work from attorneys and accountants and which may cost in the hundreds of thousand of dollars. You may hear references to "Form SB-2." This is the SEC form usually used by small businesses (revenues under $25 million) to register their securities. In addition, each state has its own set of forms and rules for registering securities.

# Regulation D

If your securities are not sold to the general public, but to a limited number or type of individuals, the offer and sale may be exempt from registration requirements at both the federal and state levels. An offer and sale of securities that meets exemption requirements is called a *private placement*. If you meet applicable requirements, you do not need to register the securities with federal or state governments. The original federal legislation in the 1930's allowed for private placements, but the rules were not well understood. In 1982, Regulation D was enacted, which made the private placement process better defined and less risky. Since then, private placements have become a common method for raising money in the private equity markets.

Regulation D ("Reg D"), which is a federal safe harbor from registration provisions, does still provide for certain kinds of controls on the issuance of securities. There are subsections of Regulation D and each is suitable for a different set of objectives and circumstances. If your offering complies with one of the subsections of Reg D, it will be exempt from federal registration. You will also need to make sure your offering is exempt from registration in every state where you offer and sell your securities.

In very brief summary, the various subsections of Reg D are as follows.

## Rule 504

The maximum amount of money that may be raised under this provision is $1 million.

In the other Reg. D provisions (described later), there are rules concerning the disclosure that must be made to potential purchasers of securities, as well as other rules concerning who may buy them. However, Rule 504 has no disclosure requirements and no investor standards. In some cases, it can be the easiest Rule under which to sell securities and the cheapest with which to comply. Some entrepreneurs refer to this as the "Friends and Family" rule, because they use this to make sales of securities to those friends and family members who sometimes are the first in line to finance a start-up business.

Despite the friendly nature of Rule 504, it has limits. Not all states have corresponding exemptions. If you are offering and selling in many states, compliance with each state's rules can be extremely burdensome for a 504 offering. (These state rules are sometimes referred to as *Blue Sky Laws*.) Also, as stated earlier, the maximum you can raise in a 504 offering is $1 million.

The Rule does not have specific disclosure requirements; but note that other securities laws require the disclosure of all material information in connection with the offer or sale of securities. Because of these anti-fraud provisions, it is highly advisable that a disclosure document be provided to all potential investors. If one is not issued and an investor levels charges of fraud against you or your company, you and your personal assets may be under siege.

Whether an offering is being conducted in accordance with Rule 504, 505 or 506 of Reg D, an *offering memorandum* (sometimes referred to as a *Private Placement Memorandum*) is almost always used to offer the securities for sale. It is the vehicle for listing the various disclosures to potential investors. These disclosures should include:

- a description of the business and its operating history for the last five years;

- a description of the products or services the business provides;

- description of the directors and officers, plus a summary statement concerning numbers of employees;

- a summary of items that may have an impact on your company's future performance. (This might include pending government regulations, expiration of patents or trademarks, and the like.);

- a summary of risk factors facing the business. (It is critical for your protection that this list be thorough. Potential risks include lack of acceptance of your product in the marketplace, loss of key employees, material downturn in demand for your products or services, unforeseen competitive pressures, catastrophic computer failure, and so on.);

- a list of highly compensated individuals in the company and their compensation;

- a thorough description of the securities being offered. (This includes voting rights, trading restrictions, warnings about the lack of liquidity in the present and future, and other technical details such as preemptive rights that could affect the securities' value under certain circumstances.); and,

- a description of the securities themselves, their number and purchase price, and whether there are any commissions given on their sale.

For a detailed description of these and other items you may want to include, see the US Government's form listing all elements of a full disclosure, which can be found at:

www.sec.gov/divisions/corpfin/forms/1-a.htm

## Rule 506

There is no limit to the dollar amount that be raised under Rule 506.

Any number of accredited investors may buy securities under this rule. The term *accredited investor* is extensively defined in Reg D. With regard to natural persons (not corporations or other entities), an accredited investor is one that has a certain net worth or a certain income and qualifies as a sophisticated investor that guarantees he or she can withstand the loss of their entire investment.

A maximum of thirty-five *non-accredited* investors can also purchase securities under this rule, as long as they are, either alone or together with a representative, sophisticated enough to weigh the risks and opportunities of the offering. The offering company usually submits a questionnaire to the potential investors to determine if they meet the guidelines.

Rule 506 requires detailed disclosure of information to potential investors if you sell to any non-accredited investors in the offering. If you are selling only to accredited investors, you do not need to comply with specific disclosure rules. However, as stated earlier, all material information must still be disclosed pursuant to other securities laws. An offering memorandum is highly recommended for your own protection.

Rule 506 is often the easiest rule with which to comply. The federal government has pre-empted the states from placing any state level requirements on the offering other than the filing of a notice of sale (Form D), the payment of a filing fee, and the filing of a "consent to service of process" (meaning you agree to deal with a lawsuit in that state, if someone should sue you). If your offering complies with Rule 506, you can be assured that it can also comply, fairly easily, with a registration exemption in every state.

## Rule 505

Rule 505 offerings may not exceed $5 million. This rule limits the number of non-accredited investors (maximum of 35), but has no investor sophistication standards. Rule 505 requires disclosure similar to that required for Rule 506 offerings. The problem with Rule 505, and the reason why it is rarely used anymore, is that there is no federal pre-emption of state level requirements for this type of offering. So, if an issuer is using Rule 505, it must find a corresponding exemption in every state in which it offers and sells. Some states may not have an exemption with which the offering can comply. In other cases, compliance with the state's exemption can be overly burdensome.

# Initial Public Offerings – IPO's

IPO's are simply another way to raise equity money for your business. Instead of offering equity to a small number of private individuals, as with private placements, the equity is offered to the public, usually by an underwriter. It is then tradable on a stock exchange such as the New York Stock Exchange or NASDAQ.

Stringent standards must be complied with in order to *go public*. All of the rules concerning disclosure mentioned above apply to public offerings. In addition, the information must first be submitted to the SEC, which will rule on your compliance to these strict standards. Each stock exchange has its own requirements as well, concerning minimum numbers of shareholders, the capital asset base of your company, and other financial thresholds before your company can be traded on their exchange.

You will need the services of an accounting firm and a legal firm to help you through this process. You will also need an *underwriter*. This is a company that will actually put your shares into the stock exchange and conduct trades. Underwriters typically are large financial firms who take a percentage of the transaction as a fee.

IPO's are complicated and expensive. They can bring enormous prosperity to a company because they provide large cash inflows. They also put the company into the public arena. Reports must be filed with the SEC at various points. An annual financial statement must be filed, as well as quarterly statements. Changes in control, acquisition or disposition of significant amounts in assets, and various other events must be reported as well. The company's officers, directors and major shareholders also have reporting obligations.

Anyone can browse through publicly reporting companies' information. The Internet has a variety of pathways into this database. An excellent one is provided by the SEC itself, and can be found at **www.sec.gov/edgar.shtml**. Choose a company that you are familiar with and look through the various reports that have been filed in the last year or so. This will give you a good idea of the reporting requirements with which public companies must comply.

# SECTION 3
## Setting-Up Your Website

# Chapter 8
## Your Website Name

## Choosing and Registering Your Domain Name

The first step in establishing a website is to choose and to register a domain name. A *domain name* is the name by which people identify and locate your website, such as www.SphinxLegal.com. A company often uses the main part of its name as its domain name. You also might consider a domain name that describes what you are selling, how you are selling it, or something along those lines. If you are selling only widgets, think about **www.widget.com** (it's taken, by Widget Group Ltd.).

To check on whether a domain name is available, go to **www.internic.net/whois.html** or **www.netsol.com/cgi-bin/whois /whois** and follow the directions. The latter site is the site of VeriSign, which used to be Network Solutions, Inc., which was the first and only domain name registrar. Now there are scores of registrars through which you can register a domain name. For a list of accredited domain name registrars, go to **www.internic.net /regist.html**.

Once you choose a domain name and determine that it is not already taken, you are ready to register the name. You do not need to have a site created or hosted in order to register the name. Just call or go to the website of an accredited domain name registrar and follow the directions. Be sure to print out any necessary instructions. Remember your password! When you register your domain name you will need to give contact and technical information. If you do not have a host yet for your website or you don't know the information for your host, the registrar will provide some temporary host information that you will need to change later.

# Cybersquatting

You may come up with a great domain name that may be owned by a *cybersquatter*. You may be able to take the name away from that owner under the *Uniform Dispute Resolution Policy* (UDRP) of Internet Corporation for Assigned Names and Numbers (ICANN). This is a non-profit corporation that manages the Internet domain name system. (Madonna was successful in taking the domain name **www.madonna.com** away from a cybersquatter under the UDRP.) You can read the policy at:

www.icann.org/udrp/udrp-policy-24oct99.htm

Arbitration is required to commence a dispute and the cost is primarily the complainant's. To succeed in a dispute under the UDRP, the *complainant* must show three things: (1) that the domain name is identical or confusingly similar to a trademark or service mark in which the complainant has rights; (2) that the domain name registrant has no rights or legitimate interests in respect to the domain name; and, (3) that the domain name has been registered and is being used in bad faith.

The first element is self-explanatory. As for the second, the policy sets forth some factors which are considered in determining whether a registrant has rights or legitimate interests in a domain name. General factors include: use of the name in a bona fide offering of goods or services; whether the registrant has been commonly known by the domain name; and, whether the registrant is making a legitimate non-commercial or fair use of the domain name without intent to obtain commercial gain by misleadingly diverting consumers or tarnishing the mark in issue. Other factors may also be considered in determining whether the second element exists.

The third element, the question of bad faith, is probably the most controversial and complicated. The UDRP provides for four non-exclusive circumstances which, if shown, will prove bad faith. These include (1) if the domain name was registered or acquired primarily for the purpose of selling, renting, or otherwise transferring the domain name registration to the trademark owner or its competitor for valuable consideration in excess of the costs directly related to registering or acquiring the domain name; (2) if the domain name was registered in order to prevent the trademark owner from using it as a domain name, provided that the domain name registrant has engaged in a pattern of such conduct; (3) if the domain name was registered for the purpose of disrupting the business of a competitor; or, (4) if the domain name registrant has used the domain name to intentionally attempt to attract, for commercial gain, Internet users to its website, by creating a likelihood of confusion with the trademark as to the source, sponsorship, affiliation, or endorsement of the website or of a product or service on the website.

The UDRP provides that the arbitrators may order the cancellation of the domain name or transfer it to the complainant. An appeals process is also provided.

There is a corresponding federal law, the *Anti-Cybersquatting Consumer Protection Act*, that provides for liability of a cybersquatter to a trademark owner if the person acts in bad faith to profit from the trademark and registers, traffics in, or abuses a domain name that is either identical to or confusingly similar to a distinctive mark, or is identical, confusingly similar, or dilutive of a famous mark.

The act provides for proceedings where an action can be filed against the domain name in the district where the domain name registrar is located, when the defendant cannot be located. The remedy to be obtained in this type of proceeding is limited to the transfer of the domain name or forfeiture or cancellation of the trademark. In a proceeding where a trademark owner personally sues the domain name owner, money damages can be obtained as well.

# Chapter 9
## Technical Decisions Regarding Your Software and Hardware

The purpose of the next three chapters is to provide guidance in securing technical services to create, expand, and maintain an Internet presence. Uses of the Internet can vary in scale. You may simply wish to start small by creating a "brochure" site, intended to display a modest amount of information and have relatively simple functionality. (Perhaps you will consider expanding later on.)

Others may see their website as a major factor in their enterprise, having a complex structure, sophisticated functions, large amounts of data, and connections with other systems, such as financial record keeping and inventory management systems.

The topics covered below are intended to provide a comprehensive description of important elements in the technical procurement process. Those who are contemplating a more modest site may not need to consider all of the items listed below in depth. No matter how simple or complex a site is intended to be, the basic steps necessary to create a Web presence are the same.

1. Define needs.

2. Examine and modify existing process.

3. Document requirements.

4. Interview and select vendors for

    a. software development and

    b. hosting, or decide to build and host the website "in-house."

5. Test functionality and response time.

6. Train users and implement system.

## Defining Your System Specifications

The creation of a set of system specifications can help bring all or most of the technology issues out for discussion, both inside the company and with potential suppliers. This exercise can serve to identify and resolve potential misalignments in goals or aspirations for the system among the company's participants. Additionally, good specifications will lay the groundwork for good technical design by identifying all major components in advance.

They also serve to ensure that a complete list of requirements is given to the technical supplier, so that the scope and costs of the project can be estimated correctly. A supplier may also be able to separate core functionality from less important "wish list" items and to identify separately the costs associated with each component.

Finally, defining and refining your system requirements in advance may drastically reduce the cost of the technical supplier. If you don't define the specifications in advance, the supplier will have to do it with you for an hourly charge. A good set of specifications may save tens of thousands of dollars in such fees.

These specifications are often gathered together and sent to various suppliers in the form of an *RFP*, or *request for proposal*. This document becomes the basis for comparing costs and items from providers. Often it becomes a part of the final agreement with the supplier and is attached as an appendix to the contract.

## Writing the Request for Proposal (RFP)

It is likely that your RFP, describing what the supplier is going to deliver, will become part of the contract. Before you embark on defining your goals in writing, review the following concepts.

## Review the process before automating

Some people have a belief that "computerizing" a process will provide improvements in and of itself. However, automating a process that should not exist in the first place just doubles the disaster.

In a recent real life example, an existing company designed a Web-based system that mimics existing workflows. Certain reports were demanded of the Web-based software that were complex and required laborious data input. However, an investigation was performed that showed that none of the recipients of the existing report actually used it for anything. It was a relic of an old process that "everybody" thought "somebody" needed. The report was eliminated and a large detour in the project was avoided.

## Automation may not be necessary to achieve your objectives

However happy the outcome in the note above, it points out the need for a process review before the specification and design of a system begins. There may be more efficient ways to organize workflow in or between departments that would bring savings and efficiencies. The cost/benefit of the system needs to be evaluated after the process changes—perhaps the system's payback was mostly related to improved workflow that actually requires no system to achieve. The extraneous report in the example above could have been identified and eliminated with no automation project.

## Be wary of using the Internet as an excuse to reorganize workflow or eliminate poor performers

A manager at a large company demanded a certain process be added to the website. In listening to the rationale, it was determined that the real problem was a poorly performing employee who could be eliminated after the system was installed. This is a poor reason to seek out automation. It is an expensive way for the manager to avoid managing.

## Know the cost of "wish list" features before demanding them

Designers of systems can get carried away with the enthusiasm generated by a new Internet project. Be sure to identify and isolate "wish list" items that are being put into the specifications. Cool features that are of minor importance can influence fundamental system design and cost disproportionate amounts of money.

An example of this occurred at a company which put clothing for sale on its new Internet website. This company was used to selling clothing through third party retailers, such as department stores, and had no direct experience selling to individual consumers. The project manager demanded that all products be available in a 360-degree view – that users be able to "spin" the products to be seen from all sides. This might have made sense with furniture or jewelry, which customers wish to examine from all sides, but not with socks or T-shirts. This feature added tremendous cost to the development, including the purchase and installation of special software, and proved to be of little or no value in generating additional sales.

# Buy Functionality and Performance, not Systems

It is a mistake to attempt to specify hardware or software by name or brand, unless the equipment needs to integrate very specifically into a certain hardware environment. Let the supplier recommend the correct environment. Make that recommendation part of the vendor evaluation.

The user (and the company) should be buying functionality and performance – the ability to do certain tasks within a certain time. Suppliers, unlike buyers, are more dedicated to keeping up with trends in the software and hardware industries. You are buying their expertise and that includes recommendations on system components.

Tests should be done against the ability to perform functions. Therefore, the specifications need to be expressed as functions. Specifying certain brand names is by definition self-limiting. That may preclude the best options.

Notwithstanding all the above, maintenance and compatibility are important issues. Software components should not be so customized or so far from the mainstream that ONLY this supplier could ever maintain the software. Expandability and spare parts should not be limiting factors in hardware selection.

# Build or Buy

Building or expanding a website poses a number of important questions concerning technology.

The elements below need to be considered when deciding whether to build the website or to outsource all of it, or some of it, to a third party. There are two basic issues to consider for each subject: capability and cost. Even if you determine that you can build your own site more cheaply and better than you could buy it from a technical supplier, you then need to ask if you want this to be the focus of your attention. The most precious resource you have may be your time. If overseeing technical development takes your attention away from building your business, make sure it is worth the trade.

## Questions to Consider

### Even if I have the technical skill now, will I be able to keep it up-to-date while I run my business?

- Will you be able to keep your skill set current at the same time you are turning your attention to starting a new business?

- Should you be devoting the bulk of your time to technical tasks, or does the new business demand that other tasks, such as sales, staffing, marketing, and the like take priority?

Does my skill set fit current industry norms, so that I can bring in outside help later on and expand my site without starting over from scratch, or otherwise interrupting my business?

- If you think you should participate or take a lead in the technical development, will you be able to smoothly hand that responsibility to others later?

- Will new programmers understand what you've done, and be able to build upon that foundation?

## Do I adequately understand the complexity of the system and website I envision?

The business owner or manager may consider hiring staff to build, maintain and otherwise care for the Web technology. In doing so, he should weigh these considerations.

## Do I know how to hire technically skilled staff?

- What criteria will I use to make certain the person's skill set fits my requirements?

- Will I know how to weed out false or exaggerated claims of technical skill?

- Can I balance the load of skill sets required for the task at hand (programmers, designers, communications, maintenance, etc.)?

## Am I willing to manage technical staff turnover?

- Will the absence of on-site staff damage my business?

- If someone leaves my firm, how will I find time to interview new candidates?

## How will I maintain continuity in the programming in the face of staff turnover?

- Can I establish and enforce programming standards and maintain detailed documentation on programs?

- Can I supervise programming staff to ensure rules are understood and complied with?

### Will my technology involve proprietary programming techniques, trade secrets, or private information concerning clients?

- Do I have policies and procedures in place to protect those items?

- Do I need to develop special contracts with my employees because of this proprietary nature?

# Hosting: In-house or Outsourced

Once your website has been designed and coded, the software needs to reside on a computer system (often a device called a *file server*) in order to actually work. Just as programs such as word processing or computer games need to be installed on a system (such as a personal computer), so a website needs a "host" system in order to function. Additionally, this host system needs to be connected to the Internet through communications lines so that users can access your website and so your site can send information to the users.

As part of the planning for an active Web presence, you need to consider whether to "host" the site yourself, on your own systems, or to hire a service to provide the hosting. Usually the service would provide the file server and all the related services needed to keep your site available to users.

### Can I provide the physical environment suitable for housing equipment?

- Do I have power supply reliability for brown outs, surges, etc.?

- Do I have access to air temperature and humidity controls in my building?

- Am I allowed access to the building on off hours, weekends, holidays?

- Can I take care of the building—for example, can I keep the wiring neat?

- Is there room to grow?

## Can I provide an environment suitable for programmers to work on complex problems?

- Have I supplied ample desk space, personal storage areas, computer systems, local area networks with e-mail and shared printers, and, dust-free and glare-free environments where they are expected to be available?

- Are there quiet work areas?

- Are there meeting or common areas that include large tables, white boards, conference call speaker phones, computer with a TV monitor with access to the local area network for programmers to get together to plan or hash out problems?

- Are meeting areas suitable for clients to meet with programmers or other staff members?

- Should I allow late night, weekend and holiday access—especially if "hosting" is part of the task?

## Are communications facilities in place to handle expected traffic?

- Will traffic exceed my system's capacity and cause slowdowns in response time or influence users' satisfaction?

- Do I have the incoming and outgoing capacity needed to handle short-term peaks?

- Am I aware of factors that influence traffic?

- Will my website see a high volume of import and export of files, especially graphics files?

- Have I considered the frequency of users' requests for new pages or new data while they are browsing through my site?

## Can I provide reliable, offsite data backup?

- Do I backup my system periodically in case of a failure in the main system?

- Is my backup stored off-site in a different physical location from the main system to guard against business interruption in case of fire or some hazardous condition?

- Is the backup copy easy to get to in case you need it?

- Does my professional hosting facility provide backup options as part of my monthly fees?

## Do I need redundant systems, so that my website is always available?

- Should I have off-site hardware backup, as well as data backup?

- How do I plan for a system to keep the website running in case of hardware, software, or power failure?

- Can I provide communications lines, a duplicate set of software and data, and a means to "switch" to the backup system?

## Can I plan adequately for future telecommunications traffic and data storage requirements?

- How do I meet peak customer demands with hardware, computation power, telecommunication capacity, and networking?

- How do I anticipate spikes in demand around certain events, like holiday shopping?

- How can I monitor and analyze traffic patterns in order to allow for adequate lead-time for planning increases to communications capacity?

- Is there software available to monitor traffic and to test the system's ability to handle future volume?

# Evaluating the Technology Supplier

Unless you are satisfied with your ability to deal successfully with the issues previously discussed, you will need to find, and negotiate with, a technology supplier. In effect, the technology supplier should have the ability to deal with all the elements discussed earlier.

In summary, the supplier should be expected to:

- Keep current with new developments in areas such as software, graphics, hardware, telecommunications, and networking.

- Provide top-notch programming and design talent.

- Provide current versions of all development and operating software.

- Provide adequate hardware and communications systems for programming, development, and operations.

- Handle the hiring and turnover of staff without interruption or damage to your project.

- Guide you to effective use of technology—lively, interactive, intuitive websites with good command of design issues.

- Have strong programming skills: no dead-ends, no mistakes, fast response times, elegant results.

- Bring good design to the screen area.

- Create a sense of continuity in the way that Web pages interact with the user and with other Web pages—the "architecture" of the site and an understanding of users' psychology as it applies to the Internet. Information organization and navigation has a dramatic effect on the usefulness of the material.

- Understand and advise on marketing issues—how to attract and keep users.

- Provide advice and solutions on having your site interact with other systems (inventory, financial, customer service, etc.)

- Create a site with scalable solutions, so that your business can grow.

- Provide security safeguards for preservation of data integrity, protection against hackers, etc.

- Be able to provide "beta" test systems for evaluating functionality.

- Plan for data storage requirements, processing power requirements, communications throughput, and other capacity constraints, for peak load conditions.

- Provide maintenance.

- Be capable of providing the next phases of growth in your system.

# Chapter 10

## Business Decisions Regarding Your Software and Hardware

### Negotiation of Hardware and Software Contracts

In order to justify the project, return must be weighed against all the system's costs over the system's life span called *full life cycle costs*. Following are some of the specific costs that comprise the full life cycle costs.

*Purchase cost.* The initial cost of hardware and software.

*Implementation cost.* The cost for the supplier to install the system, plus an assessment of internal costs—rent, power, fire code changes (if any), hours of internal systems personnel to install, training courses required, etc.

*Maintenance costs (software, content, transactions, communications, upgrades, backups, disaster recovery).* These can easily add up, over three or more years, to more than the purchase cost. Typical maintenance costs for custom-installed systems are 15-20% of the purchase price per year. Depending on the nature of the system, there are additional costs for transmitting data, for installation and use of communications lines, and for periodic backups. In mission-critical installations there are also additional costs for on-line backups, including Unstoppable Power Supply (UPS) and even a separate facility. Often there is a requirement to keep step with software upgrades, and so annual upgrade costs should be calculated.

*Support costs (users, customers).* There might be internal users who need phone support or on-site support. Therefore, overtime, sick days, coverage during staff turnover, etc., need to be included in the overall cost of maintaining the system and its users.

Systems that interact with an outside customer base (example: e-commerce websites) may need phone support customer service for outside users. This could be internal or outsourced.

*Infrastructure costs.* Installation of communications lines, rental of "cages" for equipment at off-site computer environment rental agencies, air filtration and air conditioning, fire extinguishers, power lines, special security arrangements such as door locks or card entry systems, wiring for connections of terminals, wiring for local area networks, new furniture, cubicles and walls, and other requirements need to be considered.

*Cost of integration of legacy systems, legacy data.* Some websites and the systems behind them may need to contain data on customers, such as customer loyalty, buying patterns, website negotiation patterns, and so forth. In some cases the website will represent a "fresh start," and the system can begin tracking information from the beginning of its existence.

In some cases, however, this data already has been compiled for the past. This data may be critical to the ongoing task at hand. For example, information on customers and their purchases must be maintained for marketing purposes.

Not all data is critical, however. One possible choice that may be too bold for developers to consider is to abandon the data that existed in a legacy system, except at a summary level. The cost of capturing the old detail, reformatting it, and porting it over to the new database, should be weighed against the intended use of the information.

This may take courage. For example, a company may have years of tradition, in which every nickel spent was compared to spending in previous years and previous quarters. The real value of such comparisons needs to be questioned. It may be nice to have, true, but is it worth the cost to have that information in the database? Manual retrieval (e.g. printed pages in three-ring binders) may be sufficient if there is only occasional need for the information.

*Staff costs.* New hires may be required to run the new system. Conversely, there may be savings in reduced staff requirements.

*Training costs.* Changes to the system could involve the need for training for the users and others in the company.

*Project management costs.* The need for the sophistication of the tools must be weighed in context of the complexity of the project. If specific project management tools are used, entering data on the completion level of various tasks can easily become a full-time job in itself.

## Payment Schedules

The project timetable should include well-defined milestones for completing critical achievements. The payments to the supplier should be tied to these milestones. This ensures that the project will not wander too far off track before corrections are made. It is also an incentive to the supplier.

Testing must be carefully planned so that each milestone can be accepted or rejected with some certainty that the tests reflect the viability of the system.

## Transition from Manual or Legacy Systems

Planning for the transition, including a "fall back plan" in case the transition is not successful, is a mini-project deserving separate planning. In most cases, there cannot be a cessation of business just to accommodate the transition to a new system. Therefore, planning must take into account the requirements of the business first—system second.

# Weighted Score Chart

The creation of a simple chart can help organize your thinking when comparing the services of potential suppliers.

Column 1:   The items you wish to include in your evaluation criteria.

Column 2:   The weight, on a scale of 1 to 10, given to each criterion.

Column 3:   Evaluation for the first supplier, also on a scale of 1 to 10.

Column 4:   Evaluation multiplied by the weight of each item.

Column 5 and onward:   Evaluations for other potential suppliers.

| Criteria | Weight | Vendor 1 | Vendor 1 score | Vendor 2 | Vendor 2 score |
|---|---|---|---|---|---|
| Design | 7 | 8 | 56 | 2 | 14 |
| Programming | 8 | 8 | 64 | 6 | 48 |
| Maintenance | 5 | 2 | 10 | 4 | 20 |
| Project management | 5 | 9 | 40 | 7 | 35 |
| Integration with legacy systems | 2 | 5 | 10 | 8 | 16 |
| Etc. | | | | | |
| Etc. | | | | | |
| Etc. | | | | | |
| Total Score | | | 180 | | 133 |

**For Example:**

In this simple example, each vendor's capabilities, as judged by the business owner, are weighted by the importance of that capability. The total score should give an indication of a clearly outstanding performer, or one who falls short in critical areas. This exercise is best used as an internal company tool. It is not so much a scientific exercise as it is a vehicle to make explicit the criteria that are important to the system, and that offers a way to map the vendor's strengths and weaknesses against those criteria in a deliberate, structured way.

- By soliciting each person's response to where each vendor falls in each category, a full discussion can be brought about in which all issues are discussed.

- Often a vendor can be chosen with consensus of all interested parties.

- Everyone's voice is heard.

- The best choice is easier to make.

- Agreement is achieved at all levels of the organization, helping to foster collaboration.

- A second-best supplier that has full internal commitment will provide a better outcome than the first-choice supplier if that supplier is met with suspicion, resistance, or sabotage-though-indifference.

- If no choice can be made, more data is needed or the need for the system needs to be reassessed.

# Contracts

Some business people demand written agreements for any major transaction. Some reject the idea of spending time and money on a contract when they could just get to work instead. Others do not want to get pinned down on specifying technology because they are not really sure of what they want. They want to fashion the technology "as it goes." Others think contracts are the first step towards litigation. One entrepreneur remarked, "The only time I've ever been sued has been when I've had a contract."

Ideally, you know just what your website should look like; what the software behind the screens should accomplish; and, how users should be able to navigate around the site. Ideally, your supplier knows how to deliver those things exactly the way you have them in mind. Verbal agreements can work, and fashioning the technology "as you go" can also work. It is usually safest, however, to allow this unstructured approach only after the parties have demonstrated a successful history of clear communication and understanding, coupled with prompt and excellent execution. When both parties are new to each other, however, it is probably best to define expectations, on both sides, as clearly as possible from the beginning.

A contract can range from a general agreement to a document that incorporates detailed specifications on design, functionality and performance of software and hardware. There are some dangers in either approach. The more you specify, the less input your supplier will have in doing things in imaginative, and perhaps better, ways.

On the other hand, you may not know exactly the best way to build the site. You may very much want suggestions from the technology supplier on how to accomplish certain tasks. You may have an imperfect idea of the final product. If the technology supplier is confident he or she can provide you with what you want, the supplier will be willing to go ahead with incomplete specifications. However, the more you leave in the hands of your supplier, the more you leave yourself open to surprise.

The best approach to avoid the dangers above (being too rigid or too vague) is to build an agreement that allows for frequent, step-by-step delivery and testing of components, with feedback loops and team-oriented organization.

## Your Responsibilities

You, as the buyer, should be aware of, and plan for, certain responsibilities in the development cycle. Even if you've done a great job describing your requirements in the Request for Proposal (RFP) or during the design phase of the project, you must still take primary responsibility for making sure that what is delivered is what you have defined.

This means you need to have:

- a timely review of deliverables and feedback to the designers and technicians (You may want to work out the timetable for these reviews with the supplier, so that neither one of you is wasting time waiting for the other to respond.); and,

- a thorough testing of components.

## Contractual Elements

Your contract with the supplier should cover, at a minimum, the following elements:

- system goals;

- system functions;

- performance, such as (a) the time it takes to perform certain functions, (b) the speed at which users receive a response from the system, (c) communications rates, and (d) other issues related to processing ability and data storage and retrieval, such as production of reports, system backups, and the like;

- deliverable components and a timetable for each delivery;

- cost of each component and conditions under which payments will be made (payment cycle allows time for testing, etc.);

- testing procedures for acceptance and related payments for accepted components;

- final testing of integrated components in one system;

- communications issues: specifically, capacity and reliability (guarantees on uptime and ability to connect to the website);

- planning for peak load capacity ( X number of simultaneous users);

- compatibility with other systems;

- interaction with other systems (input produced for other systems, such as inventory or financial systems, and output to be accepted from other systems, such as credit card authorization);

- future upgrades;

- maintenance issues such as data backups, telephone support and on-site support, including response times and the scope of ongoing responsibilities;

- data storage and retrieval; and,

- other critical matters, as defined in the specification process.

A set of poorly defined goals will not be rescued by a legal contract, but will instead likely be written into the contract. The lawyers will take their lead from the developers during the definition phase.

# Chapter 11
## Implementing Your Software and Hardware

A successful development plan should include a defined method of introducing the system and training those who will be involved in the processes that interact with the system. Determine strategies for the following groups.

## Users

There are a few different types of users:

- Some will actually put their hands on the system, do data entry of some sort, or create the queries for the database, or somehow manipulate the contents. Examples: purchasing systems, analytical modeling systems, and hotel or airline reservation systems.

- Some will be managers who need reports on traffic, volume, service levels, and the like.

- Some will use other systems or will be in departments that take the output of this system as input for their system or area.

- There may be clients involved who interact with the system or use it directly for purchases. For example, on-line banking and brokerages, or e-commerce on the Internet.

- Programmers are users, too.

- Some will serve as *testers*. Software and hardware need to work together according to specifications. This includes functionality and speed. Testing for acceptance needs to be well-defined and designated as a separate task.

All these persons, and perhaps more, will need to understand the system. They will be the ones judging its success.

## Introduction of System to User Community

Are the *end users* the same people who participated in specifications? Has staff or key player(s) changed? It is not unheard of for a system to be handed over, upon completion of development, to people different from those who justified and specified it. This can easily happen if the project takes more than six months to complete.

Be aware that these "new" people may not have the same desire for the system or may have confusion about its priority or their role in the new situation. Some may be worried about their jobs or their ability to perform their jobs, or about how their job definitions may change. Newcomers need to be integrated into the project.

These issues should be addressed, and not only technically. A human resources professional may need to be consulted and may wish to orient the new people on the team.

# Training, Error Control, and Feedback

A mechanism needs to be established to capture user feedback. Testing can never be 100% foolproof. Some problems may come up. This should be anticipated in the plan to avoid potential panic by the users.

## Data integrity testing

A new system may demand new types of data. In many practical instances, acquiring error-free data is the single most difficult task in system implementation. This is of particular importance if data is to be entered by the website users. For example, ordering information, shipping information, credit card numbers, and personal information can easily be entered incorrectly.

Systems that integrate orders with inventory systems and generate traditional data streams such as shipping manifests, part numbers, or other mundane information, may depend on many small details in order to work correctly. Make sure that your system does not demand PERFECT data. Do not expect PERFECT users.

Entirely new procedures may have to be implemented by suppliers who have been successfully doing business with you for years. Make sure you weigh the costs of this task, not only the burden on the suppliers' side, but also the burden on your system and staff as they work through these new procedures.

# Functionality Creep

During the development cycle, it would be almost impossible for people on the team not to generate new ideas for the system. A hallmark of system development failure is the addition of features and functions during the development phase. Changing specifications "on the fly" must be resisted. The reworking of the functionality to include new components is almost never worth the addition of an element that was not part of the original list.

However, it would be a mistake to ignore these new ideas. Some may very well contribute to a better website. A mechanism should be established to capture the new ideas as they are generated, so that good ideas are not lost, and people know their voices are being heard. These new ideas, improvements, and changes can be implemented in "Phase II."

Phase II is to take place after the current project is complete. Then all the ideas gathered during development can be considered and weighed against costs and benefits.

# Criteria for Success

Finally, determine how success will be measured. Many possibilities are available. Below are some specific questions that may be used to assess various measures of success.

- How well does the process work?

- What is the amount of improvement to the existing process?

- Will the criteria be based on user satisfaction, sales, or perhaps, customer retention?

- How will dollars be tracked?

- How do you determine if the new system has lived up to its expectations?

- Are there accounting procedures to identify dollars saved as new dollars earned?

This information provides needed feedback to the development process, provides rewards for those who deserve it, and sets the stage for further development.

# Chapter 12
## Website Content

The Internet has been heralded as a revolutionary phenomenon. It now has the ability to bring information across physical borders and into the homes of billions of individuals. It is readily available using a variety of modestly priced, standard technologies. Although it is comprised of many individual inventions, no one group or individual invented it.

The Internet is fairly reliable and naturally robust due to its decentralized components, yet no one individual or group or agency is responsible for keeping it running. And a lot, if not most, of the content available on it is available free to the Internet user. Pictures of stellar explosions taken by the Hubble telescope, details of decoded DNA, stock prices, poetry, and e-mail, are available in your living room, for free, almost instantly.

Anyone who has the ability to receive data from the Internet is not far from being able to create and publish content on the Internet, therefore contributing to the vast and expanding Internet storehouse of information. However, there is an undesirable side to free content. Everyone can be a publisher, but there are few safeguards about what might appear on your screen. The information can be of dubious quality, can be oriented towards someone's personal agenda or politics, and can be old or out-of-date.

In the United States, as in many other countries, there are certain laws that (a) ensure that you are allowed to publish content (laws concerning freedom of speech), but also (b) restrain certain types of usage of content (e.g., usage of copyrighted material without permission).

As discussed later in Chapter 15, your *trademark* or *service mark* can identify you as the author (or publisher) of the content that appears in association with your mark. Your *domain name*, a unique identifier associated with your business, is another sort of marker that identifies you as someone responsible for content.

Your website will interact with the laws of copyright in two ways. Copyright laws protect original content that goes into your site. Conversely, you are not permitted to publish someone else's material without their permission—they enjoy the same protections that you do.

# Quality of information

## Keeping content up-to-date

Out-of-date information is a recurring frustration for Web users. If you pick up an old magazine or newspaper, or last year's college catalogue, you wouldn't expect the information to be current. Very often on Internet sites, however, there is no such obvious correlation with the original publication date. Search engines may not land the user on the home page. The user may not take the path you expect, and so dates may be bypassed or simply not noticed, even if the website has them there in the first place.

If you display information that is date sensitive, make sure that it is kept current. Almost every Web user has encountered this problem. Tremendous ill will can be created when your potential customers make plans based on invalid information.

If you are starting up a new business, then an obvious consideration should be the development of a process that will keep your website current. If you are going onto the Web with an existing business, it is imperative to include your website in the list of tasks that you currently use to keep other elements in your business current.

Do not let your website be an afterthought. If you offer material for sale on the Web and neglect to update your prices when you should, you may be offering unintentional discounts to Web customers. When you update prices on the bar code scanners, menus, or advertising flyers, be sure to add your site to that checklist. If you change your hours of operation, or decide to close on the day after Thanksgiving, or remove a product line from your inventory, don't forget to update the information on your site. Carloads of clients who relied on your site to know your operating hours, now circling your store, staring at the closed doors, are soon to be ex-clients, and will no doubt tell all their friends about their disappointment.

Another common frustration is a link to a dead-end. You should periodically check to see that all of your links connect to sites or pages that are still functional. More than that, you may want to browse through those sites and make sure they still contain the sort of content with which you wish to be associated. Websites can change.

## The Data Quality Act

Some of the frustrations with the quality of information available on the Web have resulted in a recent law called the *Data Quality Act.* This Act, effective October 2002, requires the United States government to set standards for the accuracy of scientific data used by federal agencies. Under this new law, systems must be put into place that allow anyone to point out errors in the data. If confirmed, the faulty information must be removed from all government websites (and any printed publications).

While this law applies to government websites only, it is not a bad practice to provide a feature that allows your users to provide feedback and report any possible problems (such as dead-end hyperlinks). It not only provides an outlet for clients' frustrations, but enlisting the user community will help you to keep your site functional.

## FDA and FTC regulations about content

Certain agencies of the United States government such as the Food and Drug Administration (FDA) and the Federal Trade Commission (FTC) regulate information given to consumers to protect them from false or facetious claims. FDA and FTC regulations and policies concerning marketing claims are described in various acts. Some examples of these are the *Federal Food, Drug and Cosmetic Act* (**www.fda.gov/opacom/laws/fdcact/fdctoc.htm**) and the *Public Health Service Act* (**www.fda.gov/opacom/laws/phsvcact /phsvcact.htm**). Other important professional organizations, such as the *American Medical Association*, have also issued guidelines concerning marketing claims. The FDA defines standards for labeling and advertising for prescription drugs, over-the-counter drugs, food, promotional materials to health professionals and to the general public through advertising or direct mail campaigns, as well as for medical devices and materials for veterinarians.

Being out of compliance with these regulations can bring on expensive enforcement sanctions. If your website has anything to do with marketing, promotion, or sales of materials that concern any government agencies, make sure you investigate the policies governing the claims that may be legally made about your products.

## Copyright Protection

Like trademarks and service marks, *copyright* arises immediately when one creates a "work," such as a play, a book, a poem, or any other artistic or literary work. Copyright applies to many different things, including software, manuals, text on a website, recipes and more. The official categories of copyrightable matter are as follows:

- literary works;
- musical works, including any accompanying words;
- dramatic works, including any accompanying music;
- pantomimes and choreographic works;
- pictorial, graphic, and sculptural works;
- motion pictures and other audiovisual works;
- sound recordings; and,
- architectural works.

These categories are *very broad.* For example, "literary work" includes computer software programs.

Copyright *does not protect* the following:

- works that have not been fixed in a tangible form of expression (for example, choreographic works that have not been notated or recorded, or improvisational speeches or performances that have not been written or recorded);

- titles, names, short phrases and slogans; familiar symbols or designs; mere variations of typographic ornamentation, lettering, or coloring; mere listings of ingredients or contents;

- ideas, procedures, methods, systems, processes, concepts, principles, discoveries, or devices, as distinguished from a description, explanation, or illustration; and,

- works consisting entirely of information that is common property and containing no original authorship (for example: standard calendars, height and weight charts, tape measures and rulers, and lists or tables taken from public documents or other common sources).

## How Copyright Arises

Once you create something that is protectable by copyright, you own the copyright, even if you have not registered the copyright with the federal government. Owning the copyright to something means that you have the exclusive right to make copies of the work, distribute copies, perform the work publicly, display the work publicly, and prepare *derivative works* based on the original work. You also have the exclusive right to authorize others to do those things.

A copyright generally lasts for the term of the author's life plus 70 years. In the case of a work by more than one author, the copyright lasts for the term of the last surviving author's death plus 70 years.

In the case of works *made for hire*, or works made by an employee in the course of his employment (the employer is the copyright owner), the copyright lasts 95 years from publication or 120 years from creation, whichever is shorter. For certain other works, specifically those cases of anonymous and pseudonymous works, the copyright also lasts 95 years from publication.

## Benefits of Registering a Copyright

There are certain advantages to the copyright owner who has registered his copyright with the Copyright Office of the Library of Congress. First, the registration puts the copyright claim into the public records. Second, it is necessary to register the copyright for works of United States origin before one can file a copyright infringement suit in court. Third, if the copyright is registered within five years of publication, the copyright owner will have prima facie evidence of the validity of the copyright and of the facts stated in the registration certificate. (This means that in a legal action, those things will be considered proven until someone proves otherwise.)

Fourth, if registration is made within three months after publication or prior to an infringement of the work, in an infringement action the copyright owner may be able to win statutory damages (a monetary award provided by law against the infringer, without having to prove actual money damages) and attorney's fees. Finally, registration allows the copyright owner to record the registration with the Customs Service to protect against importation of infringing copies.

## Registration Procedure

Registration of copyright is cheaper, simpler, and quicker than registration of a trademark. There is no substantive review process by the Library of Congress. The copyright owner simply fills out the copyright registration form, pays the fee (at this writing, $30), and files the application with a copy of the work.

There are different deposit requirements for different types of works. If the work has confidential or proprietary information, in some circumstances portions can be blacked out or omitted. If the filing meets the procedural requirements, the copyright is registered, and the owner receives a certificate of registration back from the copyright office. The copyright office's website provides information regarding the registration procedure. It can be found at:

www.loc.gov/copyright

## Publication

If a work is "published," the law generally requires the owner to deposit the work with the Library of Congress within three months of publication. In copyright law, "publication" means:

> {t}he distribution of copies or phonorecords of a work to the public by sale or other transfer of ownership, or by rental, lease, or lending. The offering to distribute copies or phonorecords to a group of persons for purposes of further distribution, public performance, or public display constitutes publication. A public performance or display of a work does not of itself constitute publication.

Whether a work has been published may affect the duration of copyright protection, the deposit requirements, and limitations on the exclusive rights of the copyright owner.

## Copyright Notice

Regardless of whether a work has been published or the copyright registered with the Library of Congress, the copyright owner has the right to, and should for his own protection, use a copyright notice on the work. For visually perceptible works, the copyright notice should show the symbol ©, or the word "Copyright," or the abbreviation "Copr."; the year of first publication of the work; and, the name of the owner of copyright. If the work has not been published, the notice should say "Unpublished work" and state the year of creation of the work.

## Registering the Copyright to Your Website

Most websites have some level of content that is copyright protected. The website owner should give serious consideration to registering the copyright to the text and other content of his site. The procedure is simple and cheap, and can give the owner a substantial advantage in protecting his copyright. In addition, whenever you make revisions, file a separate registration. It may help you in the long run.

You may want to avoid using the United States mail to file your registration. Since 9/11/01, the Copyright Office's mail service has been severely delayed, and is not back to normal as of the time of this writing. It is best to use an overnight courier or hand delivery service instead.

## Site Content to which the Website Owner Does Not Own the Copyright

Let us say you publish a printed (paper) newsletter and sell it to your friends and neighbors. It contains articles and essays from various writers. They have all given you appropriate permission to use their work in your printed newsletter. Do you have the right to take the text of two of the pieces in your last newsletter and now put them up on your website, accessible for a small fee, without getting additional permission from the writers?

The Supreme Court says no. In the 2001 case *New York Times Co. v. Tasini*,121S. Ct. 2381, the Court ruled that where an author's work is removed from the context of the original publication and presented to readers outside of that original context, the publisher infringes the author's copyright unless specific permission is granted by the author for that use. Be sure to get specific written permission from the creator of every work that you put on your website for every particular use you plan to make of that work.

## Some Points About the Nature of Copyright

In the practice of law we have received some questions from clients concerning the nature of copyrighted works. The clients often wish to borrow an expression from a book, an article, a poem, or an advertisement. Their line of reasoning is that because the expression just has ordinary words from the English language, they should be able to use them. Some think it would it be okay to use the expression if they gave the authors a footnote, citing their authorship. However, here are the basic rules to follow.

- You can't just use others' words, even if they are words in the English language. If you want to express the same concept, do so using different words. No one can copyright "ideas" without their being in a form of expression. If you absolutely must use those words in that order, then the author of that expression has created something that is better than anything else and it is stealing to use those words without permission.

- As far as simple words of the English language are concerned, consider this expression: "To be or not to be, that is the question." Simple words in the English language, and yet most people know that Shakespeare created that line over four hundred years ago. (The reason it can be used in this book is that the copyright has expired.) Even a string of simple words can express a complex idea in a way that is difficult to improve upon. It can be tempting to "borrow," but do not.

- Finally, do not be fooled. A footnote or a citation to the author does not protect you. It incriminates you, if you do not have the author's permission to use the work. Perhaps you wrote research papers in high school or college that allowed you to quote from authors if you gave references to the original text. That is permissible under the "education" exception to the copyright laws. By putting such a citation in a commercial publication when you do not have the author's consent, you simply prove that you knew in advance you were using copyrighted material without permission.

## Copyright of the "Look and Feel" of a Website

Code behind website pages is protected by copyright under the "literary works" umbrella. If you think that another website has the identical "look and feel" as your site, you may want to investigate if a copyright violation has taken place. Likewise, you want to avoid being charged with that violation yourself.

Copyright protects against copying, so the code behind the Web pages must be copied from your code in order to make your claim. You may not simply point to the color schemes or other elements as evidence of copyright violation. In addition, the copying of the copyrighted work must be of protected expression, and not just ideas, or elements that fall below the threshold of copyright protection.

You will need to prove that someone has copied your code. You may find quirks in the code behind another website that might provide evidence of copying. Programming code is a skill that can leave patterns characteristic indicative of the programmer. However, if the exact code is not shown to have been copied outright, courts may use other tests to determine if a violation has taken place.

In addition, the copying of the copyrighted work must be of protected expression, and not just ideas, or elements that fall below the threshold of copyright protection. Items that fall below copyright protection, such as generic short phrases, are not distinguishable as being associated with a particular product or company ("Open seven days a week," "Special savings for Internet users"). Basic color schemes (blue background, white type, etc.) are not protected unless they are so distinct that users are likely to mistake your particular color palette and typeface with another company's scheme. Some colors, such as the blue that Tiffany's uses for its boxes, are copyrighted in and of themselves.

The *subtractive test* analyzes the copyrighted work, throws out the non-copyrightable elements, and compares only the copyrightable elements of the copyrighted work to the allegedly infringing work. (*Universal Athletic Sales Co. v. Salkeld,* 511 F.2d 904, 908-09 (3d Cir.), *cert. denied,* 423 U.S. 863.)

The *totality test* compares works using a "total concept and feel" standard to determine whether they are substantially similar. The *extrinsic/intrinsic* test uses a combination of objective and subjective perspectives, but both of these have largely given way to variations of the subtractive test. (*Computer Associates International, Inc. v. Altai, Inc.,* 982 F.2d 693 (2d Cir. 1992).)

An important element in the proceeding can be the determination of the intended audience. Should the tests be done from the perspective of an "ordinary user," or from the perspective of the "intended audience?" That, in turn, may depend on how narrowly the focus of the site seems to be aimed. Is it directed toward a very specific audience (art connoisseurs) or a wider audience (video game players)? (*Atari, Inc. v. North American Philips Consumer Electronics Corp.,* 672 F.2d 607, 619 (7th Cir.), *cert. denied,* 459 U.S. 880 (1982) "[v]ideo games, unlike an artist's painting,... appeal to an audience that is fairly undiscriminating insofar as their concern about more subtle differences in artistic expression.")* Narrowly focused sites that look exactly like their competition will be suspect.

# Defamation of Character

Defamation involves damage to some person's or organization's reputation. Writers of fiction and nonfiction, as well as photographers, run some risk of being charged with defamation if they portray other people or discuss organizations. Libel is written defamation. Slander is spoken defamation.

The Supreme Court reasoned, "The legitimate state interest underlying the law of libel is the compensation of individuals for the harm inflicted on them by defamatory falsehoods. The individual's right to the protection of his good name reflects no more than our basic concept of the essential dignity and worth of every human being—a concept at the root of any decent system of ordered liberty." (*Gertz v. Robert Welch, Inc.,* 418 U.S. 323, 341 (1974).)

Balancing this need to preserve reputation is the concept of freedom of speech. It is possible to curtail speech too much under the guise of protection against defamation. It is easier to defame a private person than a public one, because public people trade off their right to privacy for their fame.

Other "famous" people get less protection than ordinary private citizens, even if the person is famous against his will, for example, by being accidentally involved in a newsworthy event. The courts will attempt to balance the need for reputation against free speech rights. There are several basic elements that are required for a person to prove defamation.

1. The statement made must be defamatory, that is, it tends to harm the person's reputation, holds the person up to shame or ridicule, damages his business dealings, or makes others not wish to associate with him.

2. The statement must be false. (Truth of the statement is a complete defense.)

3. It must be about ("of and concerning") a living person or group of persons, and only these can bring the claim.

4. It must be published, and without the person's permission. The publishing must be in a form that is not ephemeral (writings in the sand at the sea shore would not qualify). Publishing the statements with the defamed person's permission is also a complete defense.

5. If the person alleging defamation is a "public figure," the statement must be published knowing that the statement was false, or the statement must have been made with a reckless disregard for the truth.

6. It must cause damage to the defamed party. If the defamation is about an organization, the statement must be explicit enough to identify the specific organization.

7. The remedy for defamation is usually money damages to the injured party.

## Showing someone in a "false light"

Another item to be aware of as a publisher of material on your site is the showing of someone in a "false light." You may say nothing directly defamatory about a person or an organization. However, if in association with other written statements or other media (such as photographs) the published material presents a negative picture of someone through suggestion, it is possible for a defamation suit to be brought against you.

For example, someone might post an article about teenage drinking juxtaposed with a picture of rowdy teens emerging from a football game. The teens in the photos may have simply been exuberant over their team's victory, but the implication is that alcohol has caused them to lose their composure. Make sure that your website does not inadvertently place a person or an organization in a questionable position.

## "SLAPP" Suits

SLAPP stands for *Strategic Lawsuits Against Public Participation*. Some of these cases have arisen when disgruntled groups have posted unflattering material about a company on a website. They might be ex-employees or others who are dissatisfied with the company in some way.

The company in question, in seeking to stop them from publishing this material, may file a defamation lawsuit. Courts have rejected these efforts to stifle public complaints as being restrictive of free speech. If the court finds this particular suit to have no basis (the remarks do not fit the qualifications for defamation), the company could face "anti-SLAPP" sanctions issued by the court, which would result in the company paying the attorney's fees for the defendant Internet speakers. (*Global Telemedia International, Inc. v. Doe 1*, 132 F. Supp. 2d 1261 (C.D. Cal. 2001). Attorneys' fees awarded were in excess of $50,000.)

Currently, different states have different anti-SLAPP provisions with varying levels of protection for companies or groups who are having unpleasant things said about them. In New York, for example, "anti-SLAPP" protections apply only to citizens posting information about public figures. In other words, the New York laws only protect citizens who post information about public figures such as politicians. The companies involved can sue for libel those people who publish derogatory material.

California's statutes, on the other hand, provide more protection for those who post the unpleasant messages. As in the case cited above, a company in California who attempts to silence criticism may, as in the above example, not only lose the case but be forced to pay the defendant's legal fees as a punishment for attempting to stifle the commentary.

# Access to Content by Minors

## The Communications Decency Act

In February of 1996, the *Communications Decency Act* (CDA) was enacted as part of the *Telecommunications Act of 1996.* The CDA made Internet transmission of indecent materials to minors a criminal offense. In 1997, the Supreme Court ruled unanimously that the CDA was an unconstitutional restriction on the Internet, a "unique and wholly new medium of worldwide human communication." The Court ruled that the regulations would reduce the constitutionally protected material available to adults "to only what is fit for children."

Responding to precedents prohibiting obscene material or talk on the radio or other media, the court said that, unlike radio, which may be playing and dispensing content to all within listening range without warning, Internet access takes a deliberate act. Also, due to the nature of the Internet, it is possible to warn viewers about indecent content. In addition, the restrictions on the nature of the forbidden material were too vaguely defined. For those and other reasons, the CDA was rejected by the Court.

## Children's Online Privacy Protection Act (COPPA)

The *Children's Online Privacy Act (COPPA)* was signed into law in 1998.

If you have a website aimed at children in particular, or even if your site would simply tend to attract children, COPPA requires the following:

- to post prominent links on your website to a notice of how you collect, use, and/or disclose personal information from children;

- to notify parents that you wish to collect information from their children and to obtain parental consent prior to collecting, using, and/or disclosing such information (with certain exceptions);

- not to condition a child's participation in online activities on the provision of more personal information than is reasonably necessary to participate in the activity;

- to allow parents the opportunity to review and/or to have their child's information deleted from your database and to prohibit further collection from the child; and,

- to establish procedures to protect the confidentiality, security, and integrity of personal information you collect from children.

To determine whether a website is directed to children, defined as being 13 years old and younger, the Federal Trade Commission, the governmental body in charge of enforcement of this law, looks at several factors regarding the site, including:

- subject matter;

- visual or audio content;

- age of models on the site;

- language;

- whether advertising on the site is directed to children;

- information regarding the age of the actual or intended audience; and,

- whether a site uses animated characters or other child-oriented features.

## Child Online Protection Act (COPA)

Congress and many individual states have passed various laws trying to regulate Internet content that may be offensive or harmful to minors. Most of these laws are being challenged on the theory that they violate the constitutional right to freedom of speech. One of these laws, called the *Child Online Protection Act*, or *COPA*, (different from the COPPA statute discussed in the previous section) makes it a federal crime to use the Web to communicate "for commercial purposes" material considered "harmful to minors" without attempts to prevent access to minors under 17, such as through an age verification device. It imposes severe monetary penalties and also possible jail time. COPA is currently the subject of a challenge as to its constitutionality. On May 13, 2002, the Supreme Court upheld an injunction barring enforcement of the statute, but sent the case back to the court that issued the injunction for further rulings on whether the law is constitutional. (*Ashcroft v. ACLU*, 122 S.Ct.1700 (2002).)

If you do have questionable content on your site you should, at a minimum, require the user to take a positive action to warrant that he or she is age 18, or 21 if that is the applicable standard where he or she lives. It would also be smart to consider requiring the user to actively agree that he or she will not redistribute the material to any minors or other persons who might find it offensive; that he or she believes in freedom of expression; and that he or she will not hold the publisher responsible for the material on the site or any material reached through links on the site.

Will this protect you from prosecution under one of the "harmful content" laws if a minor enters your site? At this point in the history of Internet law, it is not possible to predict the outcome.

# SECTION 4

## Doing Business
## on Your Website

# Chapter 13
## Selling on the Internet

Since its very earliest stages the Internet was designed to facilitate the sharing of information. Two major architects behind the initial development, the United States military and a group of universities, used networks of data lines and transmission protocols to share research and other information among their own constituents. The Internet grew out of these networks designed to communicate.

Before examining some of the basic elements needed to do business on the Internet, it may be helpful to provide some perspectives on the landscape of e-commerce.

## The E-Commerce Gold Rush

In the late 1990s, there was a frenzy of website development. Investment capital poured into technical infrastructure and software development. Many investors were frantic in their fear of "missing the boat." They were regretful later when their boats sank in the harbor before ever starting out.

There are some interesting historical parallels to the e-commerce explosion. The chronicle of two other technologies—the telegraph and the personal computer—can provide some perspective on recent events.

The telegraph, in its day, shrank the boundaries of the world like nothing before. Businessmen in California could learn of prices in New York in a matter of hours.

Telegraph companies sprang up by the dozen. Laying the infrastructure—thousands of miles of wire, with main lines branching into individual telegraph offices, at risk to the elements, floods, roaming buffalo—was a Herculean task, and an expensive one. Many start-up telegraph companies ran through their initial investments and then went out of business. After the initial wave subsided, a group of businessmen bought up several defunct telegraph companies, taking advantage of the initial investment in infrastructure. That group eventually became known as Western Union.

In the early 1980s, central processing units of computers had shrunk in size and cost to the point where they could provide computing power to individual, self-contained units at a reasonable price. The dawn of the personal computer was characterized by the development of many brands, all jockeying for position. Adherents touted the features of the PCs they liked best. When bigger companies saw that consumers were accepting the personal computer, they stepped in and soon dominated the fragmented market.

The boom-and-bust period for Internet development has gone through an exciting beginning. Some believe the 1990s formed a "first phase" of development, with a second wave of sophisticated online commercial ventures just getting ready to join in a "next phase" of development. Certainly the growth of domain names and the acceptance of the Internet as a business tool make an Internet strategy an ordinary part of many businesses today.

## The Retail Model

To many of the folks who run stores or sell brands, Internet "traffic" was irresistible. Some believed that they knew pretty much what there was to know about retail. The Internet seemed to be a place where nonstop, worldwide traffic would be walking past the door forever. E-commerce was the method to gain access to this rich market. Websites with cool functionality and displays tailored to psychological profiles would entice the users, who were ready day and night with credit cards to shop at home or wherever they might be.

Some tried to import the retail model, in its entirety, into the land of Internet traffic. A store is a separate entity from any of its neighbors. Outside the store, signage announces the store's name. Inside, a collection of brands is gathered by a buyer, who picks offerings to sell based on the store's market position, target audience, store location, and other factors. Advertising is done to help draw traffic and build brand recognition.

These virtual retail establishments, when plopped down into the Internet, did not always work according to the standard model. Traditional advertising was not effective. "Viral marketing" (an untraditional approach using email and other person-to-person methods) and other advertising techniques were deployed.

Some types of products did not take well to the Internet. Jewelry, furniture, and other products that customers wanted to physically touch were poor performers. Hackers stole information. Firewalls and other defense mechanisms were constructed to shield the website from intruders.

Some sellers, who had in the past sold only wholesale quantities, wanted to reap their long-lost profits by going directly to the consumer. The Internet was a way to do that without needing to build retail outlets. Selling directly to the consumer turned out to be harder than they thought—processing thousands of small payments, bad credit, tax collection, warehousing, inventory tracking, order preparation, customer service, special orders, fulfillment, backorders, returns, packing materials, shipping labels—wow!

## Using the Internet to Share Information

The retail model did take advantage of Internet traffic. However, the Internet's original strength was the sharing of information. The traditional retail enterprise, in part to protect its sales, and also to distinguish itself from other businesses, sets itself apart.

Are these two concepts incompatible? Perhaps not. Yet the "one-to-one" or the "one-to-many" relationships typical of retail transactions do not bring into play the "many-to-many" capabilities that the Internet makes available.

# Auctions, Reverse Auctions, Matchmaking

Other models took the Internet functions closer to the many-to-many configuration. These developers saw that the Internet was a way to bring together buyers and sellers, much as auctions did, but without the need to use a physical space to house the participants. Auctions were developed for the buyers and sellers of a wide variety of items: cargo container space, airline tickets, health club supplies, sports equipment, restaurant supplies, and from commodities such as bulk minerals to specialized objects such as Ferris wheels.

Some of these sites were technically fabulous business catastrophes. Other sites worked sufficiently well to stay in business and continue to exist today.

The auction functions did expand on information linking made possible by the Internet. However, these were fairly impersonal connections. Pure price and delivery comparisons were adequate in some situations, such as when the product is relatively inexpensive, well understood by the buyer, and will not vary in quality from supplier to supplier. Items such as books and airline tickets could often be obtained from one supplier or another, based on price and delivery only.

## Developing relationships with the customer

Business-to-business sites that used auctions or similar functions failed to create value in one important area of the business purchasing function. Professional business procurement specialists build up a trust fund of goodwill over time. The sellers get to know the buyers. Good suppliers could use their judgment to anticipate buyers' needs. Reliable buyers could count on their sales representatives to expedite special orders, help plan changes in the buyers' business, and in many ways become a partner to the buyer. Many B-2-B sites that relied solely on pricing were not successful in winning over buyers where the sales relationship was important.

The successful sites backed their offerings with good inventory and distribution channels, or sold items, such as tickets, that did not suffer from an impersonal relationship and that did not need physical delivery (like the airline electronic or "e-ticket" that requires only that an identification number be brought to the airport). And, more importantly, they worked hard to get the buyers of their goods to change traditional buying habits and try it the "new way." In many cases this took massive marketing campaigns and a good understanding of their customers.

Some of the failed enterprises concentrated their efforts on making deals with suppliers and producing technically slick websites. But eventually, they discovered that the mere existence of a site, even if it worked well, even if it had good pricing, was not enough, on its own, to get potential customers to switch away from their existing buying methods. In addition, traditional strengths in inventory management, marketing, fulfillment, and other basic business tactics were just as important as ever.

Other successful sites developed ways to generate sense of loyalty to the e-commerce customer. They used software that tracked customer preferences, either through on-line forms that customers filled out in order to freely give their preferences to the sellers, or through traditional marketing tools such as lists, home zip codes, and ongoing purchase patterns.

Systems that manage these functions sometimes are known as *ECRM* or *Electronic Customer Relationship Management* systems. Sites that ask you to "create an identity" and to "sign on" are most likely using ECRM systems. Your home address, shipping information, purchase history, and other data are used for marketing and for making customizing your visit to your needs. When you sign on to an Internet site and are welcomed with "Hi, [your name]" you know this type of software is at work behind the scenes.

These systems can track your preferences and offer up information, advertising, and choices that are more likely to fit your profile. In theory, this makes customers more satisfied with what a seller is offering, and makes customers, in turn, more loyal.

## Virtual communities

A *virtual community* is a website or collection of sites that form an online destination where people can interact, exchange information, or work and play together. These are also known as *digital communities* and *online communities*. Some virtual communities seem to have self-generated, but others were planned to a greater or lesser degree.

Examples of these communities include those formed by local sports teams; health-oriented sites where people learn about or share information on certain diseases; nation-wide groups that promote ecological issues; worldwide groups that enjoy the same hobbies or music; religious groups, and on and on. A simple search for virtual community in any search engine will reveal dozens of these entities.

This many-to-many communication conglomerate can bring together disparate individuals who share some common interest, or way of thinking, or beliefs, or goals, or all of the above. The virtual community may be a way for others to discover those things, even if they don't want to join the community. Virtual communities can, of course, engage in e-commerce along with the sharing of ideas.

# Selling on the Internet

Many of the considerations about setting up a website are addressed in Chapter 10 on contract negotiation for website development. There are some issues that relate specifically to e-commerce on the Web, however, that can be referred to separately.

Selling items on the Internet demands the same sort of business sense that selling items in a store would demand. Some of the basic considerations are listed below.

## Know What You Are Selling

Every item can be considered part of some group. Are you selling the whole group of items, or individual items? Are you selling cookies or desserts? Baseball equipment or sporting goods? This decision will affect your marketing plans, your inventory, your advertising, your customers' perception of what you are and whether to shop at your site, and is critical to effectively managing your business.

## Know Your Customers

What is the target group? Where are they located? Do they have certain characteristics that will help you serve their needs? Do they change over time? Will they stick with you as they get older, or are they replaced by new arrivals?

## Know How to Reach Your Customers

Will you advertise on traditional media? How do you know when you reach your target audience? How can you tell if they are satisfied with your goods?

Web tracking software can help analyze who visits your site and what they do while they are there. There are also methods to help drive traffic to your site.

## Provide for Customer Service

If you are starting small with only yourself or a few others, are you prepared to field questions from customers? Will you provide a telephone number for customers to call? Many business leaders recommend providing a method for customer feedback. Will you provide an e-mail address for them to use for questions? How will you monitor the quality of the responses given to your customers? Might your business grow to the point where you need full-time customer service functions?

If the answer to the last question is yes, you should note that customer service telephone response services are available. This might be more cost effective than trying to put together a dedicated customer service center on your own.

## Set the Correct Price

This is one of those basic questions that has many complicated answers. Are you bidding for contracts? Are you trying to charge the maximum possible, to make the most profit per sale, even if it means losing sales to competition? Are you thinking of charging lower prices to increase your market share? Will prices need constant adjustment to stay in tune with market conditions? How will you adjust pricing on your site? Is it a manual task, or will you be provided with a catalog of goods and services from another database? If so, will you accept that pricing, or will you mark it up (or down)?

# Creating a Check-Out Process for E-Commerce Purchases

Providing *shopping cart* holding areas in your site for customers to gather their purchases, check what they have bought, change their minds, and finalize their purchases has become routine in many websites. As discussed in Chapter 10, the processing that occurs after these choices are made can vary in complexity, depending on what you offer for sale and how it is delivered.

Some questions you might want to ask yourself are:

- Do you need to check if items are in inventory?

- If so, and not all items are available, can you process backorders?

- Should you check with the customer if backorders are okay with him or her before completing the transaction?

- Must you compute shipping charges and add them to the invoice? Are you offering different types of shipping?

- If you ship in more than one shipment, are there multiple shipping charges?

- Are your sales final? If not, how will customers return goods?

- Do I need to add sales tax?

## Collecting the Payments from Your Customers

There are two typical ways to collect payment for online purcahses. You can accept payment by check and/or credit card.

### By check

Many websites allow you the option of sending in a check for a purchase. Usually the items being purchased will not be shipped until the check has been received, deposited, and given time to clear through the bank. There are some services that will provide *check verification* if you want to reduce this time delay. The services use sophisticated algorithms to test the checking account number and the check writer's personal information against data banks of account information to determine if the check is good or not.  These services are not foolproof, but can have a high degree of reliability and may make sense in your business.

## The Credit Card Processing System

If you are selling items on the Internet, you will almost certainly have to set up a system that allows you to receive money through credit cards. You may build this process into your own system if you choose. The transactions are well-defined and should not pose a technical problem to your developers. Companies are available that can offer an entire package of services, including credit card verification and money transfers.

There are several parties involved in a credit card transaction:

- the consumer;
- the credit card issuing bank;
- the merchant;
- the merchant's bank; and,
- the acquiring bank.

The process used to authorize a credit card transaction is fundamentally the same for the different methods used to make the charge. Whether you swipe the credit card through a credit card terminal, type in the card number after receiving it over the telephone, or take the card number over the Internet using credit card processing software, the routine is similar. A different level of security usually accompanies each one of these methods. The most trusted transactions are usually those in which the credit card holder shows up personally at a store with the credit card. When credit cards are taken over the phone or on the Internet, there is a better chance that the card number is false or stolen, or that the card itself has expired.

## Internet Credit Card Authorization

For the following illustration it is assumed you have signed on with a credit card processing service.

The Internet customer decides to buy something using your website. (It is taken as given that you have a shopping cart or other method of identifying the items for sale that the customer has chosen.)

Typically, you would provide a form in which the customer can fill out information about herself, including name, address, and other personal information, along with the credit card type and the card number. Any transmission of this personal information should only be sent in encrypted form for security purposes. Additionally, the area of your site that houses this information must be secure against intruders.

Your site's credit card processing software sends the encrypted transaction to the appropriate credit card association. (The software may be in your own site, or it may be in a credit card processing service location.) The credit card association will send the request for credit card authorization to the issuing bank. The issuing bank either accepts or declines the credit card transaction. The bank's system sends this message to the card association.

The card association transmits the acceptance or denial to your credit card software. If the software is housed in the file server of a credit card processing service, the acceptance or denial will be sent to that service first, which in turn will pass the information to your site.

Assuming the transaction is authorized, your site will send the credit card processing company *fulfillment notification to permit settlement,* meaning that the goods and services have been delivered or are ready to be shipped. This means that you must in good faith actually be ready to ship the goods you are charging for in a reasonably short period of time. Each credit card issuer and credit card association will have its own rules and policies, but authorizations to charge goods or services are only valid for several days.

If the order cannot be fulfilled within that time frame, you may need to secure another authorization. In general, card issuers require that only after an order has been fulfilled are charges to be posted to the card. Check with the credit card company and merchant bank to determine what their policies are in this matter. Assuming you supply a valid *fulfillment notification,* the consumer's credit card is charged for the order. All of these transactions are usually completed within half a minute.

When you decide to close out the current series of transactions, the processing software will notify the issuing bank and the bank transfers the money into the your bank. Note that credit card companies charge a fee for each transaction, usually a percentage of the dollar amount. You will be subject to higher or lower fees depending on your history.

For example, if you provide many credit card numbers that are expired, fraudulent, or over their credit limits, and consequently are declined, your history will probably subject you to paying higher fees than if most of your credit card charges are accepted. In addition, other factors, such as the size and volume of transactions (many small dollar amounts vs. a few large dollar amounts, etc.) will affect your fee structure with the card issuers. Determine what the fee structure is with the cards you plan to process and try to get the best deal for your circumstances.

Beware of credit card setup offers you receive by email. It is best to use a service offered by a trusted source or recommended by friends or colleagues.

## Internet Taxation

State and local governments have various sales and use tax requirements. Sales made on the Internet are subject to these same regulations. Generally, states tax the sale price or rental charge of tangible personal property and certain telecommunications services sold or rented within the state. Typical state sales and use tax rules will require a seller to collect sales tax on behalf of the state under the following circumstances:

- if the seller regularly sells, rents, or leases within the state;

- buys tangible personal property or telecommunications services for resale within the state;

- acquires parts to manufacture goods for sale or resale within the state;

- has a business location within the state;

- has representatives soliciting orders for tangible personal property, or telecommunications services within the state; or,

- sells to in-state residents or businesses; and,

- delivers, repairs, or installs goods or telecommunications services within the state.

Out-of-state vendors who do any of the above will also be required to collect sales tax on behalf of the state.

The typical state sales tax plan exempts sales where the purchaser takes possession of the goods outside of the state. The sale will be exempt if the seller delivers to an out-of-state purchaser's address or to an interstate carrier for out-of-state delivery.

States and localities each have their own plans, and anyone selling or renting goods or services must thoroughly understand the laws and regulations that apply to him or her. The United States Treasury Department estimates that there are 30,000 local taxing jurisdictions, so you must assess your own situation and determine the laws that apply to you.

Many localities have attempted to compare Internet access to telephone or telecommunications services. Internet access is included in the list of things that are subject to sales tax. There is a national movement to bar this type of taxation, for various reasons.

First, utilities, unlike ISP's (Internet Service Providers—companies that provide access to or hosting of presences on the Web), are guaranteed profits. Second, regulated telephone companies, unlike ISP's, buy their access lines at wholesale prices. Third, ISP's already pay telecommunications taxes on the lines they use to deliver Internet access, so to tax ISP's like phone companies would be double taxation.

In addition, some localities have attempted to enforce overly broad sales tax laws on Internet sellers. For example, Vermont has attempted to require any out-of-state company running an *electronic mall* to collect taxes on all sales made to Vermont residents, even if the computer server hosting the electronic mall is not physically located in Vermont.

To keep localities from taxing Internet access and from attempting to broaden their sales and use tax plans to unfairly target Internet sales, Congress enacted the *Internet Tax Freedom Act* in 1998. It was recently extended to remain in effect until November of 2003. The Act prohibits state and local governments from taxing Internet access fees, except for those states that had been doing so prior to October of 1998. Those states may continue to do so only if they can show that the taxes had been generally imposed and actually enforced on Internet access providers before October 1, 1998. Some states have voluntarily agreed to abide by the national moratorium even though their tax schemes could meet this exception.

The authors have noted frequent confusion about this Act. The Act does not exempt purchases made on the Internet from sales tax. The Act does put a moratorium on multiple and discriminatory taxes on electronic commerce. This means that state and local governments are barred from imposing taxes subjecting Internet buyers and sellers to taxation in multiple states. It also bars them from attempting to tax commercial transactions on the Internet that have no comparable offline equivalent.

As explained above, state sales taxes are levied on sales only when the buyer and seller are in the same state, or the seller has a sufficient connection with the state in which the buyer resides. Sales at a retail store to a local purchaser are clearly subject to the sales tax model. Sales made by phone or mail order are more difficult to determine. Usually, the law requires that the seller must have some sort of *physical presence* in a state for there to be sufficient cause to collect sales taxes. This might mean a branch office, a salesperson, a warehouse, or the like.

Logically, taxation of Internet sales should follow the same rule as taxation of sales made by phone or mail order. And, in most places, it does, thanks to the Internet Tax Freedom Act. Be sure to check and comply with your local sales and use tax rules and regulations before you start selling goods or services on the Internet.

# Chapter 14
## How to Attract Visitors to Your Website

If you are reading this, you probably do not need to be convinced that a lot of people use the Web and that access and usage are increasing daily. It is probably safe to assume that over 500 million people use the Web and that most of them have at least a moderate amount of education and means.

Some people may use the Web for very limited purposes, such as to look at stock prices. Others use it to get information about anything and everything. You can research the best camera for the money you have to spend. You can find out about resorts and what they offer. You can make plane and train and hotel reservations. You can compare prices. You can read books, do all kinds of research, and buy almost anything. Many people start their searches for goods and services on the Web.

The number of registered Internet dot-com domain names is growing. It is now considered a normal part of business practice to have a Web site, no matter how mundane the business may be. All the talk of the "bursting of the Internet bubble" notwithstanding, there are more domains now than ever, and they are growing in number faster than ever. Several sources show more than 30 million individual dot-com domain names registered.

In addition, other categories, such as dot-net, are also expanding. These figures imply two dynamics: there will be more sites for your site to compete with, but there will be more people ready to look for you and use your site when they find it. So, once you have a website, you need to get people to find it and use it.

# Search Engines

Some people may look at your website because of a word-of-mouth, or word-of-email, referral, or a direct email campaign you may undertake. But most people will get to your website through a search engine.

People use particular search engines for different reasons. Some people are just used to one search engine so they keep using it. Others are on America Online (AOL) and do not even know how to go to any other search engine other than the one AOL happens to use.

## Getting Your Site Listed on Search Engines

Some search engines are directories compiled by humans. Some of the most important directories are Yahoo, LookSmart, and the Open Directory. Yahoo charges a fee to list commercial categories. To be listed in Yahoo, you must go to the site and go through the steps at "Yahoo Express" to be listed. To submit to LookSmart, commercial sites must also pay a fee. At the time of this writing, LookSmart provides the main listings used by the Microsoft Network search service, which is widely used. You can choose "Basic Submit" or "Express Submit." A third directory, the Open Directory, allows commercial sites to submit for free, but there is no guaranteed turnaround time nor an answer about whether you have been accepted.

Be sure to think carefully about the description of your website that you submit to a directory. The editors do not like marketing hype and could reject your listing, even if you paid the fee.

Other non-directory search engines *crawl* the Web and pick up your website information whether you want them to or not. Some of the well-known crawlers are *Google, Inktomi, FAST, Teoma* and *AltaVista*. You can submit your site directly to most of these crawlers by going to their websites. Some also have a fee-based listing service which will guarantee your listing and get you listed much more quickly than waiting for them to crawl to your site.

Google also has a paid listing (advertisement) option. The paid listings appear above and beside the regular search results. There are also paid listings available in Overture (previously *GoTo*) and *FindWhat* (both *pay-per-click* search engines).

You can do the work of submitting your site on a regular basis to these sites yourself or you can hire one of the myriad consultants and companies offering this service. Beware of email offers, however. Email appears to be the breeding ground for a whole new collection of scammers. It is best to get personal recommendations for these services from friends and colleagues.

Submitting to the search engines is an ongoing task; not a one time activity. You must set aside time or money, or both, if you want to get the most traffic to your website. It is wise to check your listings and resubmit if necessary at least once every few months. You should treat the cost of submitting to search engines as a necessary start-up cost for your business, just like stationery and telephone lines.

There are various ways to structure your website for optimum placement in search engines. *Meta tags* can be included in the html code on your site and will help with search engines that support meta tags. For example, many search engines recognize *description* and *keyword* meta tags. If you include these meta tags, with a good description and good key words for your site, this can help searchers locate your site using certain search engines.

Building links within your pages and putting important key words and phrases near the top of relevant pages of your website can also increase your standing in search engines. You should also avoid using frames, and consider synonyms and variations on your key words that should also be included in your text. Try to use key words and phrases that your prospective customers would use in conducting their searches for goods and services.

Also try to get related sites to add links to your site. Some search engines count the number of links that point to your site and use that in determining how high you place on their resulting lists of found sites. (Your competitors will not want to add links for your site, of course.) More detailed information on these strategies is readily available on the Internet. Just go to any search engine and look for "search engine placement."

One way of improving your marketing efforts is to track the traffic to your website. Tracking mechanisms can be built into your website by the developer or you can often get traffic reports from your hosting service. The reports can tell you things such as the site your visitors jumped from to get into your site; the site they went to afterwards; and, how long they stayed at your site. These reports can also tell you what path your visitors chose as they went through your site and how long they stayed on each individual page.

These elements can be critical in evaluating the effectiveness of your site's "information architecture." Different trackers will provide different information. You can use this information to pinpoint your marketing efforts.

# SECTION 5
## Intellectual Property
## Basics for Your Website

# Chapter 15
## Trademarks and Service Marks

---

*Trademarks* and *service marks* help to protect you and your company when doing business on the Internet. If you think of a catchy name for your products or services, you will want the consumer who remembers that name and looks for it later to come to you, not to your competitor. The trademark laws are designed to protect the consumer from purchasing "knock-off" or "copycat" goods or services. If a jacket says "L.L. Bean" on it, the consumer should be confident that it was actually made by (or for) L.L. Bean.

## Trademarks

A trademark is unique identifier for your product. A trademark can be a word or several words, or can be a logo or symbol. The symbol can stand by itself or be used in conjunction with words. In special cases, colors and even sounds have been held to be valid trademarks. The government keeps a list of trademarks that are registered and approved by them as being acceptable, but in theory and in practice, trademarks exist the moment you start to use them in commerce.

# Service Marks

A service mark serves the same purpose as a trademark, but denotes a service rather than a physical product. Consulting is a service, for example, as opposed to dishwashers or cars. So, consulting firms would have service marks, while product manufacturers use trademarks. (For the balance of this discussion, we will address trademarks, but the concepts apply equally to service marks.)

## Trademarks and Service Marks versus Patents and Copyrights

Trademarks and service marks protect the names or identifying symbols or logos of goods and services. Patents and copyrights should not be confused with each other or with trademarks and services marks.

Patents protect inventions. If you think you have an invention that could be the subject of a patent, you should get a book on patents. You should also consider consulting a patent lawyer. Patent law is very complex and is usually only undertaken by specialists in that area.

Copyrights protect original creative works, such as artistic, literary or musical works. Copyrights are addressed in Chapter 12 of this book.

## The Purpose of Trademark Protection

It may come as a surprise to many business owners that the purpose behind the government sanction and protection of trademarks is to protect the consumer, not the business owner. The touchstone of trademark law is *consumer confusion*. Legitimate marks help consumers distinguish one product from another. That this protection also extends to the owner of the mark is secondary to the goal of preventing consumer confusion.

Misunderstandings about the fundamental nature of trademarks have caused business owners to miscalculate their abilities to protect their trademarks. Often, in fact, the trademark may not be held as valid or protectable by the owner because it fails the consumer confusion test.

Two of the bases on which the United States Patent and Trademark Office (USPTO) may refuse registration are that the mark is "generic" or "merely descriptive." An illustration may help explain the meaning of these terms.

**For example:**

> You could not register a trademark for the word "pumpkin" when you are selling pumpkins at a pumpkin stand. This identification does not help the consumer distinguish your pumpkins from anyone else's, because the word is the generic, or common, name for the item you are selling.

> However, if you decided to name a brand of shoes "Pumpkin Shoes," then most likely you will be granted the trademark registration, because as of yet no one else has used the word to name their line of shoes. Also, the phrase is neither generic nor merely descriptive. Therefore, the consumer will find that trademark helpful in identifying your shoes from any other shoes. A brand name for shoes such as "Brown Leather Shoes" would not be registrable, because it is merely descriptive of the product and not distinctive.

This applies to services as well. If you run a design studio, you will not be granted a registration for the service mark "The Design Studio," even if you have those words on letterheads and business cards. You could probably get a registered service mark for "Pumpkin Design Studios," if you wished, because it will alert the buyers of those services that the origin of the work is from your studio alone.

## Using the trademark symbols ™, ˢᴹ and ®

You may start using the ™ trademark symbol (or ˢᴹ for service mark) from the very first day you start using the mark in commerce as a claim to the public that you own the mark. You may not use the ® symbol until your registration is granted by the USPTO.

## Benefits of registering a trademark

It is not necessary to register your trademark with the federal government in order for you to be able to protect it legally, because rights in a trademark arise simply from use in commerce. However, federal registration does give various benefits to the owner of the mark.

First, it provides constructive notice nationwide of the trademark owner's claim. If the owner has to initiate legal action to protect the mark, the federal registration will provide clear evidence of ownership of the trademark (although ownership of the mark is not exempt from challenge simply because of registration). In addition, the owner may bring legal action in federal court, rather than state court, which can be advantageous. Registration can also be used as a basis for obtaining registration in foreign countries. And, registration may be filed with the United States Customs Service to prevent importation of infringing foreign goods. So, although registration is not necessary, it can assist the owner of the mark in various ways in protecting his rights in a mark.

States also have their own registration processes, for those owners who don't see the need to register federally. This would be the case if your business would always remain completely local and you would never sell anything outside of your state.

## The federal trademark application process

The United States Patent and Trademark Office (USPTO) reviews trademark applications to see if they meet the standards for "registration" into a national system of trademarks. Only after a trademark is "registered" may you use the registration symbol ®.

An application must include the following elements before the USPTO will accept it:

- name of the applicant;
- name and address for correspondence;
- clear drawing of the mark;
- listing of the goods or services; and,
- filing fee for at least one class of goods or services.

If your application does not meet these requirements, the USPTO will return the application papers and refund any fees submitted. Depending on whether you are filing on an "Intent to Use" basis or are already using the mark in commerce, you may also need a *specimen* of use of the mark on the goods, or describing the services. A specimen is something evidencing the mark as used in commerce, such as a photograph of a jar of jelly with your label and trademark on it.

The USPTO classifies the mark into certain categories based on the goods or services you are selling. Therefore, you must specify the product or service category on which you are using the mark or on which you plan to use the mark. If one trademark is used to identify, for example, a type of dishwashing liquid, the same mark might be registered in another product category (tools, for example) without causing consumer confusion. Therefore, product categories define market limits for registration of the mark.

The USPTO also decides whether your trademark application adequately describes, in plain English, what it is you are selling and what the mark is intended to identify. If your claim is too broad or not specific, for example you want to register a certain mark for use on "all products manufactured in this facility," it will be rejected. If your claim is too narrow, it may be found acceptable by the USPTO, but it may be very limited in the products for which it will be registered. For example, a clothing trademark might be specified for use on pants, which is fine, but if you had claimed the mark as one to be used on other specific clothing items such as shirts, then your use of the mark on those other items would be registered as well.

The USPTO is not a trademark police force. It does not guarantee that you have the right to use the mark. It will not search the world for other marks that may come along that look like your mark in order to protect your interests. It is up to the owner of a mark to enforce its rights in the mark. A letter to the alleged infringer may initiate enforcement of rights. It may progress to a full-blown lawsuit, but in any event, it is the owner of the mark who must be vigilant in making sure the mark is not copied or misused.

## Registration process

You do not need an attorney to file a trademark application. The application process is specific in its demands and you must follow the rules in order to register your mark successfully. The USPTO will provide friendly advice but will not act as your representative in the filing process. It is up to you to get it right. There are several books that can guide you through this process. You may also apply for registration using the Internet. The Trademark Electronic Application System (TEAS) is available at:

www.uspto.gov/teas/index.html

## A working example

Trademark law can be confusing. An example of what types of marks may or may not be registrable may help you understand this area of the law.

Let us say two people, Tammy and Susan, manufacture apple juice. Tammy's juice comes from her orchard and is tart. Susan has another sort of apple orchard and her juice is sweet. Both come to market in big barrels. Consumers who wish to purchase apple juice at the market would not be able to tell which type of juice they were getting without opening a barrel and tasting it, because both barrels look the same.

Tammy now starts labeling her juice barrels with the word "Juice." She likes the idea, and decides to apply for trademark registration for her product. It is her product, after all, and it is juice, so why not register that trademark before someone else does?

Her trademark application would be denied. She has merely used the generic name of the product. The labeling of the barrel with the word "Juice" does not help an otherwise unknowing consumer identify the juice as Tammy's juice. The trademark office would reject the trademark as being "generic."

Susan decides that she would sell more juice if people could distinguish her juice from anyone else's juice. She decides that "Sweet Orchard Apple Juice" would be a good name, and starts stamping those words on her barrels. She, too, wants trademark registration for her label.

Susan's application would also most likely be denied by the USPTO because the words are "merely descriptive" of the item she is selling. Someone else may start making sweet apple juice, and he or she should not be precluded from using those descriptive words on his or her label.

Susan might propose using "Susan's Sweet Apple Juice." This is the type of mark that has a good chance of registration. It is neither generic nor merely descriptive. First, the USPTO would check that no one else has registered the phrase "Susan's Sweet Apple Juice," and if no one has, she could have her mark registered in the category of "light beverages." The basis for the registration is to assist Susan in preventing imitators from fooling the consumer. The mark can also hurt Susan's business. For those who do not like sweet apple juice, the mark helps them avoid a product they do not want. If Susan has a bad crop one year, people may avoid her juice from then on.

Suppose someone else named Susan starts making apple juice. Could she register her own name for her own apple juice? No! Why? Because it would be the basis of consumer confusion! The second Susan is out of luck. The only way the second Susan could register the mark is if she could prove that *her* trademark was in use in interstate commerce before the first Susan's mark, "Susan's Sweet Apple Juice," was in use.

Rights in a trademark begin the moment the mark is used in commerce, whether it is registered or not. Registration does give the owner of the mark certain legal benefits, as described above. Could the Susan who first used her name on the apple juice stop the second Susan from using her registered mark? Possibly, if they were competing in the same markets, such as the same city or geographical area.

# Chapter 16

# Publishing Law, Copyright, and Electronic Media

## Trademarks Identify the Speaker on the Internet

Many companies are establishing a presence on the World Wide Web, with the company's trade name prominently displayed on the site's *home page*. The company may be surprised to learn that it has just ventured into the publishing business and that mass media law governs some of its activities.

The Supreme Court has denoted different *categories* of speech. Trademarks may be characterized as a certain kind of speech, and may also identify a particular speaker as the "source of speech" on the Internet. Both points are important in determining:

- what degree of protection the speech has;

- what causes of action may be brought against the speaker; and,

- what defenses are available to the speaker.

## Different speech receives different protection

*Editorial content* is one type of speech, and it demands full protection from the First Amendment. (*Miami Herald Publishing Co. v. Tornillo*, 418 U.S. 241 (1974).)

Advertising is classified as *commercial speech*, and the Supreme Court says that the Constitution accords a lesser protection to commercial speech than to editorial. (*Central Hudson Gas & Electric Corp. v. Public Service Commission of New York*, 447 U.S. 557 (1980).) Nevertheless, the Constitution affords *some* sort of protection to commercial speech, even if it is a lesser one.

Fully protected commercial speech *does* exist. Speech does not lose its First Amendment protection merely because money is spent to announce it, as in a paid advertisement of one form or another. (*Virginia Pharmacy Bd. v. Virginia Citizens Consumer Counsel, Inc.*, 425 U.S. 748, 761 (1976).) The Supreme Court said in 1977: "*The listener's interest {in commercial speech} is substantial: the consumer's concern for the free flow of commercial speech often may be far keener than his concern for urgent political dialogue. Moreover, significant societal interests are served by such speech.*" (*Bates v. State Bar of Arizona*, 433 U.S. 350 1977).) The Court recognized that people are interested in reading advertising and that freedom of speech applies to commercial speech.

The Court has said, however, that there is lesser protection available when the "expression relates solely to the economic interests of the speaker and its audience." (*Central Hudson Gas & Electric Corp. v. Public Service Commission of New York*, 447 U.S. 557 (1980).)

To summarize there is:

- editorial speech that is fully protected, within the limits proscribed by the Supreme Court (e.g., obscenity is not protected);

- commercial speech that is fully protected; and,

- commercial speech that is less protected.

## Different speakers have different responsibilities

As will be seen in examples to follow, courts have used some basic models to characterize the speaker in various situations involving printed or spoken words.

*The Publisher:* The publisher owns the original contents and is responsible for controlling the contents. The publisher also exercises control over areas in the publication that are "rented" to others for advertising purposes. The publisher may choose who will advertise and may also refuse to carry advertising. In most cases this would be the company that owns the Internet site. The more *control* one has over what goes onto the site, the more likely that person is to be held legally liable for claims regarding those contents.

*The Distributor:* The distributor (or *common carrier*) is one that acts as a "mere conduit" between publishers and the public. It does not review contents or necessarily know what the contents of the publications are. This might be the group that provides hosting for your site and also the telephone line or communications supplier. The distributor is least likely to be held liable for the published contents on a site because it has *no control* over those contents.

*The Individual:* Anyone may exercise First Amendment rights by printing information. (*City of Ladue v. Gilleo,* 114 S.Ct. 2038 2d 36 (1994).) Exercising those rights subjects one to the possibility of liability.

*The Anonymous Individual:* Sometimes, you do not know who is speaking. The First Amendment does protect anonymous speech. The Supreme Court upheld the right to write, print and distribute leaflets with no identification of source. (*Talley v. California,* 362 U.S. 60 (1960).)

However, magazines must, by law, file the name of the publisher with the United States Postal Service, and, if an advertisement's trademark is not obvious, the publication must "mark all paid reading matter 'Advertisement.'" If there is no trademark identifier, magazines in effect have to substitute a "generic" trademark (the word "Advertisement").

## Advertisements have their own type of speech

Advertising as a term is constantly changing as new media and marketing techniques emerge. It may be said that anything carried by media with a trademark is presumed to be advertising. The Food and Drug Administration (FDA) defined advertising in 1995 to include "all commercial uses of the brand name of a product (along with or in conjunction with other words), logo, symbol, motto, selling message, or any other indicia of product identification. ..." (60 Federal Register 41314.) Trademarks imply advertising, which implies commercial speech, the type of speech that may receive less constitutional protection.

## Commercial Speech on the Internet

There is ordinarily no question in the reader's mind whether a given page of a magazine, or a section of a given page, contains editorial content or advertising content. A trademark usually identifies the area as advertising and therefore as commercial speech. However, there can be difficulty discerning between the two when moving from page to page on the Internet due to lack of context. A magazine's pages are physically bound together, which implies that all pages contained therein come from the same publisher. In addition, to state the obvious, one knows from experience and through the design of the magazine that one page is distinct from another.

None of these conclusions follows necessarily for a website's contents. It may be hard to know when you are moving from one page to a new page or using a hyperlink to go to an entirely different website. In both instances the user/reader clicks on icons or text, but the resulting page can be from an entirely different source than the previous one.

Imagine if you were looking at a printed magazine, and the act of turning a page could transform the publication in your hands into an entirely different printed product made by a different publisher and even printed in another country, and whose contents may be a few minutes, or a few years old. This can happen to a surfer on the Internet.

This lack of context intensifies when geographic-based trademarks encounter the global network. (*Kenneth Sutherland Dueker, Trademark Law Lost in Cyberspace: Trademark Protection for Internet Addresses, 9 Harv. J.L. & Tech. 483 (1996).*)

A United States Court convicted an Italian publisher for trademark infringement when it published a magazine similar to an existing United States magazine (the Italian *Playmen Magazine* vs. U.S. *Playboy Magazine*). Italian courts did not agree, and allowed the magazine to be published in Italy, which it did for several years. Later, a website in Italy was found to have violated a United States court's injunction when the Italian website made the magazine's contents available. However, the magazine's mere presence on the Internet was not the focus of the court's reasoning. Rather, the court found that the fact that the Italian website allowed entry only if it received a subscription payment and then issued a password to the user, implied that the Italian publisher was reaching out to sell the enjoined publication to United States readers. (The Italian publisher had unsuccessfully maintained that visiting the website was comparable to getting on a plane and flying to Italy.) (*Playboy Enterprises, Inc. v. Chuckleberry Publishing, Inc.,* 79 Civ. 3525 (SAS) (1996 U.S. Dist. LEXIS 8435).)

## Identifying the Speaker on the Net

Creation and maintenance of registered domains on the Internet is a way of grouping and identifying the type of contents to be found on successive pages. In addition, a domain is useful in identifying the "speaker," who is responsible for the content contained within the domain. In the real world, different organizations in different lines of business may use the same trademark as long as the mark is distinguishable by lines of business (an example might be Sphinx Publishing and Sphinx jewelry.) On the Internet the domain name "www.Sphinx.com" would be available to only one of these product makers—the first one to register. An Internet user would need some other clues to know which one (if either) of the companies the site represented.

### Responsibility of the domain owner

The owner of a domain may be held responsible for its contents even if the owner did not enter the contents (for example, if chat rooms or bulletin boards allow users to enter content).

Two likely causes of action for contents published on a website are:

- infringement of copyright and,

- libel, or character defamation (writing something untrue that is damaging to someone's reputation).

The domain owner must be wary of publishing contents that may subject him to these types of claims.

# Infringement of Copyright

Briefly, copyright protects someone's creative work, and can be used for writings, music, and paintings. You may not use someone else's words, music, art, or other creative work without their permission. Even if you attribute the work to the correct author, if you publish work on your site without the author's permission, you may be held liable for copyright infringement.

The distinct combination of color palette, typefaces, and other graphic elements of a site are often referred to as the "look and feel" of a website. This "look and feel" has been held as copyrightable and you must not use a combination of elements that would make a user mistake your site for some other site. A good analogy would be to think of the cover of a magazine – each magazine strives to create a look and feel to their covers and usually they are quite distinctive. If one magazine makes its covers so like another magazine's cover that it would be mistaken for the same publication, it is an infringement of copyright. The same idea applies to websites.

A few decisions by the courts on these matters can give you an idea of the issues in this area:

&#x1F4D5; A subscription bulletin board service infringed a magazine's copyrights by distributing copyrighted photographs, even though the bulletin board operator did not know that the photographs had been uploaded (*Uploading* is the transfer of a file from a user's computer to a host computer through telecommunications lines) by subscribers onto the bulletin board. (*Playboy Enterprises, Inc. v. Frena*, 839 F.Supp. 1552 (M.D. Fla. 1993).)

📖 A bulletin board operator was found liable when users uploaded plaintiff's computer game programs onto the service so that other users could copy the games instead of buying them from plaintiff's company. (*Sega Enterprises, Ltd. v. Maphia*, 30 U.S.P.Q.2d (BNA) 1921 (N.D. Cal. 1994).)

📖 An online service that had numerous bulletin boards available to over two million subscribers was held to be *similar to a newspaper* and liable for statements made by a bulletin board subscriber, because it held itself out as *exercising limited editorial control over the contents of its bulletin boards.* It was held to be analogous to a newspaper and therefore a "publisher" of its contents, even though a subscriber had written the defaming statement. (*Stratton Oakmont, Inc. v. Prodigy Services Company*, 1995 WL 323710 (N.Y. Sup.) (1995).)

📖 Another bulletin board operator was found not to be liable for defaming statements found on its service. The rationale behind the decision was *lack of editorial control.* The court was explicit: "*{the provider} has no more editorial control over such a publication than does a public library, book store, or newsstand, and it would be no more feasible for {it} to examine every publication it carries for potentially defamatory statements than it would be for any other distributor to do so....*" (*Cubby Inc. v. CompuServe Inc.*, 776 F.Supp. 135 (S.D.N.Y. 1991).)

# Using the Publisher Model

Courts have likened domains and websites to printed periodicals. ("[T]he Internet may be likened to a newspaper with unlimited distribution and no locatable printing press...." (*U.S. v. Baker,* 890 F.Supp. 1375 (1995).)) In the past, printed materials have received the strongest protection of the First Amendment and safeguards have been weaker where the broadcast media are concerned. Thus broadcasters have been held responsible for identifying the speaker when airing political campaign endorsements. (*Loveday v. Federal Communications Commission,* 707 F.2d 1443.) However, the restraints on broadcasting have relied on the "scarcity of bandwidth" rationale that cannot be said to apply to the Internet. (*Red Lion Broadcasting Co. v. FCC,* 395 U.S. 367 (1969).)

The endorsement by a publisher ("Good Housekeeping Seal") of an advertising claim in the publisher's magazine made the publisher liable for negligence when the product advertised injured a reader. (*Hanberry v. Hearst Corp.,* 81 Cal. Rptr. 519 (Cal. Ct. App. (1969).) Not all advertising in a magazine is treated as being endorsed by the publisher. However, advertising has been held to make the publisher liable for injury *when the publisher should have known the product being advertised was dangerous,* even though the publisher did not create the contents (soldier of *Fortune Magazine* case). So, beware of advertising you accept for publication on your site.

## Implication for Internet Hyperlinks

*Hyperlinks* are elements that serve to bring a user to another Web page or to other Web resources. Hyperlinks can be text links, images, buttons, or other elements in a website. The "buy" button that brings a user to the checkout portion of an e-commerce site is a typical example of a hyperlink. Often text links are underlined to distinguish them from ordinary text. Depending on the settings of your computer, your mouse pointer on the screen may change shape when it points to a hyperlink – for example, the pointer may change from an arrow to the image of a hand, indicating that the user may click on the link to be taken to a new destination.

Hyperlinks can be and are commonly established without reference to the domain name of the linked-to site. (*Intermatic Incorporated v. Dennis Toeppen,* 1996 U.S. Dist. LEXIS 14878.) A hyperlink for a map of Greenwich Village might lie behind the words "Greenwich Village." A hyperlink to a catalog of products might simply have a representation of the catalog, which, when "clicked" will activate a hyperlink.

The fact that you may have a hyperlink to another website does not mean that your contents and the linked contents are considered to be one and the same. If your website contains nothing but e-commerce catalogs, but has references to another website that has political speeches, the information on the website with the trademark does not become a political speech, too.

However, the United States Supreme Court has also stated the reverse proposition: informational literature does not turn into commercial speech simply because the published piece contains advertising for related products, even if the publisher was economically motivated for producing the piece. (*Bolger v. Youngs Drug Products Corp.,* 463 U.S. 60 (1983). Court concluded, nonetheless, that the material in question in this case—informational flyers promoting prophylactics—were commercial speech because other evidence, including concession of the publisher, supported that conclusion.) Consequently, it is most likely that your own content will speak for itself. It will neither be tainted nor can it borrow the characteristics of linked contents.

## Summary

Trademarks on the Internet, either in domain names or website pages, identify a person or a group as responsible for creating or delivering the contents. Different models used to characterize the owner of the domain or Web page (publisher, distributor, individual, anonymous) imply differing amounts of responsibility for the contents. The applicability of these different models to the Internet remains uncertain in the courts, because the cases to date have almost all involved other media.

A website's contents may be classified as commercial or noncommercial speech. If the trademark implies the content is commercial speech, the contents receive a certain type of protection, usually less than full First Amendment protection afforded to noncommercial speech. Trademarks usually identify commercial speech, but organizations may associate their mark or name with noncommercial speech. However, linking commercial speech in an indirect way to a current news topic does not by itself transform commercial speech into editorial speech.

The use of trademarks on the Internet therefore has important implications for the owners of those marks. The entrepreneur who develops a Web presence must be mindful that use of trademarks and service marks, and the publication of content on a website, all carry potential liabilities.

## The Publisher Model in Action

The various regulations and responsibilities in media law can present a complex set of variables to the publisher. A working example, given below, will highlight some of these variables and demonstrate how a well-meaning Internet publisher can invoke several aspects of mass media law in the ordinary course of business.

The Chefs Club
**November Update**
Eating through the Web™
*We here at CC are chefs who love to dine and cook. This is our monthly guide. See inside this month for new recipes from:*
**Greenwich Village restaurants**.

"Visit the Sphinx Bar for the nation's best jazz!

*hyperlink*

Website for the Sphinx Bar in Chicago, Illinois

## Hypothetical

CC, a club for dues-paying members organized in Wisconsin, decides to put up a website guide offering monthly updates on where and where not to eat. To help defer costs, CC decides to rent out some of the space in its popular site to restaurants and nightclubs, offering hyperlinks to those that also have websites. The consultant that CC hires to design the site also takes the ads over the telephone, and takes an ad from, and enters the Internet Protocol Address for, the Sphinx Bar in Chicago, Illinois. The Sphinx Bar in New York's Greenwich Village sues CC for trademark infringement.

## Response

Defenses for CC include positioning itself as the publisher of a periodical. In the case of *It's in the Cards, Inc. v. Fuschetto* (23 Media L.Rptr. 2082 (Wis. App. 1995)) a posting of private information on an Internet bulletin board located in Wisconsin invoked a state law requiring that libel claims against newspapers and periodicals be brought to the attention of the periodical, and the periodical be given an opportunity to retract the statement, prior to commencing suit.

The court determined that the plain meaning of "periodical" meant a publication that is published at regular intervals. Because the bulletin board service in this case posts messages at irregular intervals, it did not qualify as a periodical, according to the court. However, in CC's case, since CC's Internet offering is published monthly, it should be qualified as a periodical under Wisconsin law. Therefore, by law, The Sphinx should be required to offer CC a chance to retract before bringing suit.

A second line of defense for CC is to move to dismiss for "lack of personal jurisdiction." In *Bensusan Restaurant Corporation v. King,* (96 Civ. 3992 (SHS) (1996 U.S. Dist. LEXIS 13035) the owner of the New York City Blue Note nightclub sued a Columbia, Missouri nightclub of the same name for trademark infringement, but only after the Missouri club created a "Blue Note" website. The court dismissed the case, saying that the New York club's allegations were insufficient to support a finding of "long-arm jurisdiction," which would give the party with the grievance the right to sue someone from out of state on the aggrieved party's home turf.

The court reasoned that even though a New York resident could find the site and gain access to it:

- the user would have to own a computer, have Internet access, and take affirmative steps to access the site;

- the person would have to call the Missouri box office in order to reserve tickets to the club; and, finally,

- the user would have to go to Missouri to get the tickets and see the show.

Even if the person was still confused, the confusion would be occurring in Missouri, not New York.

However, the court maintained that "the mere fact that a person can gain information on the allegedly infringing product is not the equivalent of a person advertising, promoting, or otherwise making an effort to target its product in New York." This implies that the inclusion of the hyperlink *in an article about Greenwich Village* might be construed to have been intentional advertising "in New York."

This brings us to CC's third line of defense: although the referenced hyperlink appeared in its periodical, it was a paid advertisement and therefore, as long as CC was not aware of any falsity or implied falsity, the plaintiff must look to the advertiser for relief, if any. In *Yuhas v. Mudge*, (322 A.2d 824 (N.J. Super. Ct. App. Div. 1974) the court concluded that a magazine had no legal duty to the public unless the magazine guarantees, warrants or endorses the product. *"To impose the suggested broad legal duty {to investigate advertisements} upon publishers of national circulated magazines, newspapers and other publications, would not only be impractical and unrealistic, but would have a staggering adverse effect on the commercial world and our economic system."* (ibid. at 825.) Also, in *Hernandez v. Underwood*, (7 Media L. Rptr. 1535 (N.Y. Sup. Ct. 1981) the court held that Newsday had no duty to investigate each of the advertisers who purchase space in its papers. Requiring media to investigate every ad is unrealistic and impractical, said the court.

The weak spot in this line of argument is the lack of notice that the hyperlink was an advertisement. There was no notice that the hyperlink was part of a paid notice. The publishers were free to disown the ad's contents, but the website visitor does not realize that the contents were not put forth by the publisher, which may be misleading. It may be held to imply endorsement, in which case, as in *Hanberry v. Hearst,* (81 Cal. Rptr. 519 (Cal. Ct. App. 1969) the publisher does assume some liability.

Finally, Section 43(a) of the Lanham Act 15 U.S.C. Section 1125(a) explicitly provides that publishers and broadcasters of advertisements that violate Section 43(a) will not be liable for damages provided that they are "innocent violators." (15 U.S.C. Section 1114(2)(B).) If CC can maintain its position as publisher, this should exonerate it.

Beware what you put on your site. It is best to consult an attorney if you are sued or threatened with suit because of content or links on your site.

# Conclusion

Over the last few centuries, legislatures and courts have developed specific rules (negligence standards, for example) for dealing with every sort of business situation. One example relates to the mailing of letters by ordinary mail; complicated rules govern the time at which offers are deemed to have been made or responded to, by outlining every possible sequence of mail-and-reply combinations that can happen through standard mail, using postmarks as a guide for the sequence. As use of communications over the Internet becomes standard, rules will develop that will govern all the new Internet parameters. Authentication of email contents, mailing times and receipt times will be called for as a means of self-protection.

Business on the Internet can be rooted in the same legal and financial basics as any traditional brick and mortar enterprise. At the same time, certain features of the Internet can bring you face-to-face with legal aspects of the business world that some companies never have to face, and some only face when they are well established. These issues, such as mass media law, computer law, and intellectual property law, can be a lot to handle in addition to forming the right kind of company, getting financing, and dealing with sales, marketing, inventory, contracts, and human resource issues. Done correctly, dealing with each of these areas can put real strength behind your new company.

We see these laws continuing to evolve to embrace Internet-based transactions. As a business owner, you need to keep current on the nature of the rules governing your Internet transactions.

# The Future Prospects

We see a few basic things happening in the near future:

- internet becomes standard business tool — acceptance of e-commerce in all commercial transactions;
- internet used as an adjunct to existing businesses;
- internet changes business, but does not displace traditional businesses;
- international use generates new possibilities;
- increase in the numbers of websites and users; and,
- novelty decreasing, reliability increasing.

# Standard Business Tool

Your clients, investors, and suppliers will come to expect a website for every business. (Some already do.) Your employees will rely on Internet access and email in the ordinary course of their workday. Email letters and their attachments will carry business information, contracts, orders, specifications, and every other facet of business.

# Marketing

Increased numbers of websites and increased numbers of users who expect a Web presence and e-commerce facilities have already made an impact on the business community. As the novelty of the Internet wears off and users refine their skills, usefulness will become the key parameter in their choice of where to go to get the services they need. You will need to maintain your Internet presence and constantly be vigilant about competition and your user community.

# Opening Up International Possibilities

The Internet is comprised of many individual inventions, but no one group or individual invented it, and no one group controls it. It is fairly reliable and naturally robust due to its shared components, yet no one individual or group or agency is responsible for keeping it running. We won't speculate as to the Internet's ability to change the world, but it is going to be added to the forces of social change, for good or ill. Because of the Internet's decentralized nature, traditional political boundaries are relatively small barriers to Internet information.

In business terms, in the future the Internet will bring widening access to international markets. Traditional boundaries may not stop the retrieval of information, but they can stop goods and services from flowing. Care has to be taken when entering the international arena. Tariffs, duties, international shipping charges, and monetary exchange rates may all need to be added to your profitability equation.

Different laws govern other countries. You will be subject to those laws in your efforts to collect money and to guard your intellectual property. International standards and agreements are being developed in some of those areas – for example, the *World Intellectual Property Organization*, or *WIPO*, presents a forum for trademark and patent protection in over 100 member countries worldwide. However, not every country on earth is a member. Additionally, policing the use of your intellectual property rights, and enforcing violations of those rights is still up to you, individually.

Once you are on the Internet, you are part of and subject to worldwide access, automatically. That means you should make yourself aware, periodically, of developments in international business relations and their implications for your business.

# This Is Only the Beginning

The Internet has engendered a lot of discussion as to its future. We believe the Internet has just begun to have its impact felt on our society and the world at large. Children born today may find it hard to imagine a world without it, just as we can sometimes today take telephones and radio for granted. Understanding the Internet's evolution and potential while conducting a profitable business will take initiative, money, patience, dedication, mental energy and common sense.

We hope that you find our guide helpful in clearing your path to success.

# Glossary

---

## A

**accredited investor**. A natural person (not a corporation or other entity) that has a certain net worth or a certain income that guarantees that he or she can withstand the loss of his or her entire investment.

**Anti-Cybersquatting Consumer Protection Act**. Federal law that provides for the liability of a cybersquatter to a trademark owner if the person acts in bad faith to profit from the trademark.

**articles of organization**. *(See certificate of organization.)*

**assignable contract**. A contract that assigns to someone other than the signing parties the responsibility for the performance of the contract.

**auctions, reverse auctions.** On-line auctions use the same concepts that apply to real life auctions—offering something for sale and receiving bids on the item, with the item going to the highest bidder. Reverse auctions allow a potential buyer to name a price that buyer is willing to pay. That price is made available to potential suppliers through the website. If one of them is willing to sell the item for the named price, the sale is made.

**authorized shares.** After the number of shares is decided upon, that number is noted in the company formation documents. The maximum possible shares described in those documents are the authorized shares. Not all authorized shares need be issued. However, at any given time, the shares "issued," not authorized, represent 100% of the ownership of the company.

# B

**B-2-B.** *(See business-to-business transactions.)*

**basis of property.** Purchase price of specific property.

**bulletin board service.** A website that allows third parties to post information on the site. Some bulletin board services monitor, and may edit, the submitted material, sometimes by screening out offensive words. Others simply provide the website as a medium of exchange among contributors and do not have any control over the content.

**business-to-business.** B-2-B transactions are those in which one company sells products directly to another company, for resale sometime later on, possibly after additional work is performed.

**B-2-C.** *(See business-to-consumer.)*

***Business-to-Consumer.*** When a retailer sells individual items to a customer, such as in a department store or a grocery store.

**buy-sell agreement.** *(See shareholders' agreement)*

# C

**C corporation.** One of the types of entities under which you may do business and achieve the protections of limited liability. That is, the liabilities incurred by that business would be in most cases limited to those assets owned by the company. In other words, someone who wins a lawsuit against the corporation cannot take the owner's personal assets.

**capitalized, adequately.** The corporation has a sufficient amount of assets to meet its reasonably foreseeable needs without placing one's personal assets at risk.

**certificate of organization.** The document that demonstrates the organization of a corporation.

**Communications Decency Act (CDA).** The Communications Decency Act (CDA) was enacted as part of the Telecommunications Act of 1996. CDA made Internet transmission of "indecent" materials to minors a criminal offense. In 1997, the Supreme Court ruled unanimously that the CDA was an unconstitutional restriction on the Internet.

**Child Online Protection Act (COPA).** The Child Online Protection Act or COPA, (different from the COPPA, that follows) makes it a federal crime to use the Web to communicate "for commercial purposes" material considered "harmful to minors" with severe monetary penalties and also possible jail time.

**Children's Online Privacy Protection Act (COPPA).** If you have a website aimed at children in particular, or even if your site would simply tend to attract children, COPPA requires you to post information on how you plan to use information you gather. It also requires you to notify parents of your plan to collect the information. The act has several other requirements intended to safeguard children 13 years of age or younger. This Act was signed into law in 1998. It remains law as of this writing, but has been ruled unconstitutional by the Third Circuit and will receive Supreme Court review.

**convertible note.** A variation on an ordinary loan, this note allows the lender the option of converting all or part of the loan to equity based on certain formulas.

**copyright.** The legal right granted to an author, composer, playwright, publisher, or distributor to exclusive publication, production, sale, or distribution of a literary, musical, dramatic, or artistic work. This allows the copyright's owner to prevent a copier from using the copy or copies, and compensatory damages under certain conditions.

**corporation.** A body that is granted a charter recognizing it as a separate legal entity having its own rights, privileges, and liabilities distinct from those of its members. Corporations are entities created by the state in which they are formed.

**cybersquatting.** The registration and use, in bad faith and for profit, of someone else's trademarked name as a domain name. The intention is often to sell the domain name to the trademark holder at exorbitant prices.

# D

**defamation.** The act of maliciously injuring the good name of another. The information must be false and must injure the person to whom it refers. The injury could be nonspecific, that is, it could injure the person's reputation generally.

**distribution of property.** A tax differentiation that deals not with salaries or dividends, but with the assets owned by the corporation.

**domain name.** A series of letters used to name organizations, computers, and addresses on the Internet. Every computer on the Internet has an "address" which is a series of numbers much like a telephone number. (In technical jargon that address is called the Internet Protocol or IP address.)

# E

**Electronic Customer Relationship Management (ECRM) Systems.** The name given to computer software that is used to track a company's relationships with its customers. Names of customers are linked to information about such basic things as the customer's address and phone number, and also to information on the company's products and sales. ECRMs may also provide automatic responses to email questions, allow for online, real time customer service "chat sessions" in lieu of telephone conversations, and have other features that reduce and manage customer call volume. These systems also may house information about existing contracts with various clients, display pricing options for clients, and prompt the company at certain times.

**encrypted transaction.** For certain transactions a computer program scrambles (encrypts) the message into a code that is unscrambled (decrypted) by the receiving computer, which by pre-arrangement has the "key" to the encryption code used to send the message. If a website has a provision for credit card sales, most often encryption is used to protect the information.

**equity investment.** This occurs when someone invests in your company by buying shares of stock.

# F

**fair use.** Copyrighted material is protected against those who would make copies for their own use without payment to the copyright owner. However, there are certain exceptions called *fair use* exceptions. One example of fair use is for education. A teacher is permitted to make copies of material for use in the classroom. Generally, there is no fair use exception available to the typical website owner that allows him or her to use someone else's material.

**fictitious name certificate**. A document that is filed with the local government (town, city, county, or state, depending on where you live) that puts the public on notice that you are an entity doing business through a "trade name".

**fulfillment notification to permit settlement.** This is part of the sequence of transactions that occur when someone makes a purchase on a website using a credit card. After authorization for the purchase is given by the credit card issuing bank, the seller informs the bank that he or she is ready to actually fulfill the order, that the goods are in stock and can be shipped, or that services being purchased are about to be delivered or have been delivered to the buyer. Credit card issuing companies usually have their own individual sets of rules governing the time frames involved.

# H

**host system.** The computer where the Web pages and content of a website reside. This can range from a single personal computer to a large complex network of computers.

**html.** Hypertext Markup Language. A language used to structure text and multimedia documents and to set up hypertext links between documents used only on the World Wide Web.

**hyperlinks.** Strings of letters (and possibly, numbers) that lead you automatically to a Web page when you click on the link with your keyboard or mouse. The Web page may be another page in your own website or may be in a different website.

# I

**infringement of copyright.** Making copies of copyrighted material without permission of the holder of the copyright. Gaining permission may involve the payment of royalties to the copyright owner or the owner may freely grant it.

**Internet Corporation for Assigned Names and Numbers (ICANN).** The non-profit corporation that has responsibility for the IP address space allocation, protocol parameter assignment, domain name system management, and root server system management functions previously performed under U.S. government contract by IANA (Internet Assigned Numbers Authority) and other entities.

**Internet Tax Freedom Act of 1998.** This act prohibits state and local governments from taxing Internet access fees, except for those states that have been doing so prior to October of 1998.

**intranet.** A privately maintained computer network that can be accessed only by authorized persons, usually members or employees of the organization that owns it.

**Initial Public Offering (IPO).** The first time a corporation offers its stock to the public, or "goes public."

**Internet Service Provider (ISP).** A company that provides other entities and individuals with access to, or presence on, the Internet. Most ISPs are also Internet access providers; extra services include help with design, creation and administration of World Wide Web sites, training, and administration of intranets.

# J

**joint venture.** A partnership, usually one formed for a specific project.

**judgment.** A determination of a court of law; a judicial decision.

# L

**libel.** A false publication, as in writing, print, signs, or pictures, that damages a person's reputation. Libel is a type of defamation.

**limited liability company (llc).** A legal entity with characteristics of both a corporation and a partnership. The tax treatment of an LLC is similar to that of a partnership. That is, the income is not taxed at the entity level, but at the equity owner level. But the LLC also has the benefit of limited liability, meaning that the owners are not personally liable for the business's debts and obligations. Its limited liability protection is similar to that of a corporation.

**limited liability entity.** An entity whose equity owners are not personally liable for the entity's debts and obligations, such as a corporation, LLC, limited liability partnership, or limited liability limited partnership.

**limited partnership.** In a limited partnership, there are one or more general partner(s), who do not enjoy limited liability status, and one or more limited partners, who do. The limited partners cannot participate in the running of the entity's business, or their limited liability status will be jeopardized.

# M

**meta.** An element, with the tag name of "META," expressing certain key information about a given HTML document. The META element can be used to identify properties of a document (e.g., author, expiration date, a list of key words, etc.) and assign values to those properties. It is used by search engines to help categorize web pages.

# N

**non-compete provisions**.   A part of an employee agreement (contract) that provides for the security of proprietary information if and when the employee moves on to other job opportunities.

**nonprofit corporation**. An entity recognized as a legal "person" that is set up to run an operation in which none of the profits are distributed to controlling members.

# P

**parent company.** A company that owns and controls one or more other companies, which are called *subsidiaries.*

**partnership.** An arrangement between two or more persons who agree to pool talent and money and share profits or losses for the purpose of undertaking some sort of business.

**pay-per-click search engines**.  This is one way to pay for advertising through a search engine in order to get "targeted traffic".  Sites vary in how they set up account "balances" or the way they charge.  Basically, you set up key words that are important for your site and you pay the search engine when a user searches on the word(s) that you have selected.  The more you pay, the higher up on the search results your site will be listed.

**Project Evaluation and Review Technique (PERT).** A method, using diagrams, where flowcharts work responsibilities in a complex project so that all tasks stay coordinated and bottlenecks can be foreseen and avoided. In addition, the effects of changes in the project plan can be readily evaluated.

**piercing the corporate veil.** Holding the equity owners of a corporation or limited liability company personally liable for the company's debts and liabilities. This is a legal remedy that can be used to obtain assets of a company's shareholders or equity owners to satisfy a judgment against the company. A court will only allow the piercing of the veil in limited circumstances. Some of the factors which may lead a court to pierce the veil are commingling of personal and company assets; failure to observe company formalities; failing to hold oneself out to the public as a limited liability entity; undercapitalization; use of company assets for personal purposes; and, failure to make legally required filings.

**private placement.** An offer and sale of securities by an entity to a limited number or category of persons.

**professional corporation.** A corporation owned and run by certain professionals such as accountants, lawyers, or doctors. Most states allow certain professionals to incorporate only as a professional corporation. Although the corporation does have limited liability status, it does not protect the professionals from malpractice liability nor does it alter professional responsibility or privilege.

# R

**request for proposal (RFP).** This is a document that is sent to various suppliers in order to develop a basis for computing costs relating to specific items, services, concepts, etc. that a supplier will provide.

# S

**scalable.** Capable of being expanded in size or function without having to alter existing structure or mechanisms.

**S corporation.** A corporation that has made an official election under federal law to be treated similarly to a partnership for purposes of tax law. The tax attributes of the corporation flow through to its equity owners and are taxed only at the owner level. This is called "flow-through" taxation.

**secured loan.** These are loans that are backed by collateral, which are assets of some kind that the lender will obtain if a loan is not paid back.

**service mark.** Any word, name, symbol, device, or any combination, used, or intended to be used, in commerce, to identify and distinguish the services of one provider from services provided by others, and to indicate the source of the  services.

**shareholders' agreement.** An agreement among shareholders governing the sale or other transfer of shares, and usually including what happens if a shareholder working for the corporation leaves the job or is fired, or dies or becomes disabled.

**shares.** When a corporation is formed, it is divided into parts called shares. The number of shares that comprise 100% of the company can vary. In theory, there could be only one share, owned by one person, which would comprise 100% of the company. More often, the corporation is formed with multiple shares, which can range from a small number (often 200 shares) to a large number (50,000,000 shares or more).

**shopping cart.** On a retail website, a function which "holds" the items you have selected for purchase until you are ready to complete the order.

**slander.** A false statement, not in writing, that damages a person's reputation. Slander is a type of defamation.

**sole proprietorship.** A business owned and managed by one individual, not incorporated, and not having limited liability status. The owner of a sole proprietorship is personally liable for the business's obligations.

**Strategic Lawsuits Against Public Participation (SLAPP).** Civil complaints or counterclaims (against either an individual or an organization) in which the alleged injury was the result of petitioning or free speech activities protected by the First Amendment of the United States Constitution. SLAPPs are often brought by corporations, real estate developers, or government officials and entities against individuals who oppose them on public issues. Typically, SLAPPs are based on ordinary civil tort claims such as defamation, conspiracy, and interference with prospective economic advantage.

**subsidiary.** A company that is managed and owned by another company, the *parent.*

**subtractive test.** A "legal" test that is used to analyze a copyrighted work by eliminating the non-copyrightable elements and comparing only the copyrightable elements of the copyrighted work to the allegedly infringing work.

# T

**totality test.** A "legal" test which compares two works using a "total concept and feel" standard to determine whether they are substantially similar.

**trademark.** Any word, name, symbol, or device, or any combination, used, or intended to be used, in commerce to identify and distinguish the goods of one manufacturer or seller from goods manufactured or sold by others, and to indicate the source of the goods. A brand name.

**trademark dilution.** Use of a trademark by one other than its owner, in a context where there is not a likelihood of confusion to the public, but where the use of the trademark by the subsequent user will lessen the uniqueness of the prior user's mark and thus weaken the mark.

# U

**underwriter.** A specific company that puts shares of your company into the stock exchange and conducts trades.

**Uniform Dispute Resolution Policy (UDRP).** This is the policy that governs the resolution of disputes over domain names.

**unsecured loan.** Loans that are not backed by collateral and are much riskier for the lender.

**The United States Patent and Trademark Office (USPTO).** The USPTO is an agency of the U.S. Department of Commerce that grants patents for the protection of inventions and registers trademarks and service marks. Its website has additional information and can be found at **www.uspto.gov**.

# V

**virtual community.** A website, or collection of sites, that is used or visited by people or entities sharing similar beliefs, values, interests, disabilities, etc.

# W

**website architecture.** The infrastructure of a website, how it looks and functions, how the user interacts with it, and all the components that go into its structure and how it works.

# Appendix A

## Basic Legal Concepts with Business Implications

This list serves as a quick reference for important legal concepts that might affect your Internet business. Through this list you can easily locate information on the ownership of your software, the UCITA (an e-commerce statute), and contracts used in your business. The legal concept regarding each is listed first, followed by the impact it may have on your business. There is also information that you can quickly reference on lawsuits that might arise from your business contracts, including the basic legal procedure involved and the major issues that might arise.

## Ownership of Software

*Legal Note*

- Copyright belongs to the creator, unless the creator is an employee, or the work is otherwise done as "work for hire."

*Business Implications*

- If the creator is an employee of the company (or other employer) and does work "within the scope of his or her employment," the work is "work for hire" and the copyright belongs to the company (or other employer).

- If the company buys the time of the creator as "work for hire," for example by contract with the programmer as a consultant, the company owns the copyright to the software.

- Company may use, sell or license the software.

*Legal Note*

- Work for hire other than by an employee  is ALWAYS through a written agreement, never implied or assumed.

*Business Implication*

- You should have a work-for-hire contract ready to use with contract programmers.

*Legal Note*

- Even if the company develops the software from scratch, if the process is patented by a different entity, the company cannot use or sell it. (Example: one-click checkout process patented by Amazon.com cannot be used by others even if they write similar one-click checkout software themselves.)

## Contracts

*Legal Note*

- Verbal and written contracts are both valid.

  *Business Implication*

  - Even if there is no signed contract, a contract may exist by way of the parties' oral statements, or even by their behavior (e.g., performance and payment).

*Legal Note*

- Contract law

  *Business Implications*

  - If there is no signed contract, the agreement between the parties is governed by state or federal law, depending on the subject matter. Many general contract principles are outlined in the Uniform Commercial Code (UCC) adopted by many states.

  - There is an extension of the UCC called "UCITA" which specifically applies to electronic commerce (see below).

*Legal Note*

- Contract law model
  (Performance - Cost of Performance = Profit)

  *Business Implication*

  - In the majority of computer-related contracts, the buyer is entitled to "performance" done in a "workmanlike" manner according to "industry standards."

*Legal Note*

- Buyer protection

  *Business Implication*

  - If performance is lacking, or substandard, or late, the buyer may recover damages because of the provider's failure to perform. Damages may be limited in whole or in part by your contract language.

*Legal Note*

- Seller protection

*Business Implication*

- If the buyer fails to pay, or cancels midway through the project, ordinarily the contractor / performer is entitled to the profit he would have made, minus any savings due to the cancellation, unless unusual or offsetting circumstances exist.

## UCITA

*Legal Note*

- Proposed guidelines for e-commerce transactions, which have been adopted by many states

*Business Implications*

- Primarily defines the buyer/seller relationship in an e-commerce transaction.

- Some attorneys specialize in UCITA and related concepts.

## Contract Lawsuits

*Legal Steps*

- Prove existence of agreement.

- Prove breach of agreement (failure of one side to perform or pay).

- Prove damages due to breach (loss of profit, damage to business).

*Legal Process*

- Complainant files suit with the court (unless an arbitration or mediation provision applies).

- Defendant answers the charges to the court, and perhaps makes counterclaims against the other party.

- Period of "discovery" (oral and /or written questions from the each side to the other, which must by law be answered truthfully). "Depositions" are these discovery interviews.

- Legal "briefs" are submitted to the court by each party. Briefs are legal arguments explaining why a party should prevail.

- Trial.

- Expense.

  - Timeframe for this process: 1–5 years

  - $5–10,000 retainer common

  - $20–100,000 legal fees not unusual

  - Time and attention of management

*Legal Alternatives*

- Mediation—Non-binding attempt to compromise.

- Arbitration—Binding (usually; depends on arrangement between parties) ruling given by arbitrator, but no explanation of reasoning is given. If binding, no appeal possible, and the decision will be enforced by courts.

*Legal Problems*

- Determine breadth of problem.

- Estimate damages.

- Estimate costs.

- Identify business implications

  - Legal fees.

  - Time away from business.

  - Reputation in industry.

- Get legal opinion.

- Determine course of action.

# Appendix B
## Sample Business Worksheets

Use these sample worksheets to start and run your business. Feel free to copy all or parts of these worksheets, or modify them to fit your individual needs. We hope that they give you valuable ideas and will serve as a way for you to get started in finding what methods work best for your own financial, technical and business needs.

### Table of Worksheets

# Financial Worksheet

page 1

| Monthly P&L | Year 1 Month 1 | Year 1 Month 2 | Year 1 Month 3 | Year 1 Month 4 | Year 1 Month 5 | Year 1 Month 6 |
|---|---|---|---|---|---|---|
| *Revenue* | | | | | | |
| Item or Service 1 | | | | | | |
| Item or Service 2 | | | | | | |
| Item or Service 3 | | | | | | |
| Item or Service 4 | | | | | | |
| Item or Service 5 | | | | | | |
| **Total Revenue** | | | | | | |
| *Cost of Sales* | | | | | | |
| Parts, components | | | | | | |
| Sales commissions | | | | | | |
| Inventory | | | | | | |
| Shipping | | | | | | |
| Other | | | | | | |
| Other | | | | | | |
| **Total Cost of Sales** | | | | | | |
| *Detailed Expenses* | | | | | | |
| Compensation | | | | | | |
| Bonuses | | | | | | |
| Benefits | | | | | | |
| **Total Salaries and Benefits** | | | | | | |

## Financial Worksheet

page 2

| Monthly P&L | Year 1 Month 1 | Year 1 Month 2 | Year 1 Month 3 | Year 1 Month 4 | Year 1 Month 5 | Year 1 Month |
|---|---|---|---|---|---|---|
| **Marketing and Advertising** | | | | | | |
| Advertising Expense | | | | | | |
| Direct Mail Campaigns | | | | | | |
| Conventions & Shows | | | | | | |
| Research Material | | | | | | |
| Travel | | | | | | |
| Customer Service | | | | | | |
| **Total Marketing & Advertising** | | | | | | |
| **Monthly Infrastructure** | | | | | | |
| Rent | | | | | | |
| Electric, other utilities | | | | | | |
| Website Communications | | | | | | |
| Website Hosting | | | | | | |
| Phone (local and long distance) | | | | | | |
| Cell Phone/Pagers | | | | | | |
| Office Supplies & Misc. | | | | | | |
| Stationery & Business Cards | | | | | | |
| Postage and delivery | | | | | | |
| Insurance | | | | | | |
| **Total Monthly Infrastructure** | | | | | | |
| **Professional Services** | | | | | | |
| Legal Fees | | | | | | |
| Accounting Fees | | | | | | |
| Consultants | | | | | | |
| **Total Professional Services** | | | | | | |

## Financial Worksheet

| Monthly P&L | Year 1 Month 1 | Year 1 Month 2 | Year 1 Month 3 | Year 1 Month 4 | Year 1 Month 5 | Year 1 Month |
|---|---|---|---|---|---|---|
| **P&L Summary** | | | | | | |
| **Total Revenue** | | | | | | |
| *Subtract:* | | | | | | |
| **Cost of Sales** | | | | | | |
| **Gross Profit** | | | | | | |
| *Subtract:* | | | | | | |
| **Salaries & Benefits** | | | | | | |
| **Marketing & Advertising** | | | | | | |
| **Monthly Infrastructure** | | | | | | |
| **Professional Services** | | | | | | |
| **Total Expenses** | | | | | | |
| Corporate Reinvestment | | | | | | |
| Debt Payments | | | | | | |
| **Net Profit** | | | | | | |
| **Basic Cash Flow** | | | | | | |
| **Net Profit** | | | | | | |
| *Subtract:* | | | | | | |
| **Capital Expenditures** | | | | | | |
| Office Build-Out | | | | | | |

## Financial Worksheet

page 4

| Monthly P&L | Year 1 Month 1 | Year 1 Month 2 | Year 1 Month 3 | Year 1 Month 4 | Year 1 Month 5 | Year 1 Month |
|---|---|---|---|---|---|---|
| Office Equipment | | | | | | |
| Office Furniture | | | | | | |
| Computer Hardware | | | | | | |
| Communications Devices | | | | | | |
| Software | | | | | | |
| Phone System | | | | | | |
| Other Capital Expenses | | | | | | |
| **Capital Expenditures** | | | | | | |
| **Cash after Capital Expense** | | | | | | |
| *Add:* | | | | | | |
| **Investments/Loans** | | | | | | |
| **Cash Balance** | | | | | | |

# Technical Budget Worksheet

page 1

**Staffing**
**In-House Technical Staff**

| Department/Position | Annual Salary | Year 1 1st Qtr | Year 1 2nd Qtr | Year 1 3rd Qtr | Year 1 4th Qtr | Year 2 1st Qtr | |
|---|---|---|---|---|---|---|---|
| **Customer Service** | | | | | | | |
| Director | | | | | | | |
| Phone support rep | | | | | | | |
| Technical support rep | | | | | | | |
| **Marketing** | | | | | | | |
| Director | | | | | | | |
| Research | | | | | | | |
| **Technical Operations** | | | | | | | |
| Programming | | | | | | | |
| Hardware | | | | | | | |
| Graphic Designer | | | | | | | |
| **Content Management** | | | | | | | |
| Editor | | | | | | | |
| Editor | | | | | | | |
| **Advertising Management** | | | | | | | |
| Director, Advertising | | | | | | | |
| Ad sales | | | | | | | |
| Advertising Analyst | | | | | | | |

## Tech. Budget Worksheet

page 2

| Staffing In-House Technical Staff | | Year 1 1st Qtr | Year 1 2nd Qtr | Year 1 3rd Qtr | Year 1 4th Qtr | Year 2 1st Qtr | |
|---|---|---|---|---|---|---|---|
| **Department/Position** | **Annual** | | | | | | |
| | **Salary** | | | | | | |
| **Technology and Operations [8]** | | | | | | | |
| Director, Internet Technology | | | | | | | |
| Director, Internet Operations | | | | | | | |
| Manager, Technical Administration | | | | | | | |
| Operations Technical Administration | | | | | | | |
| Operations Technical Team Lead | | | | | | | |
| Technology and Operations Support | | | | | | | |
| Director, Information Services | | | | | | | |
| LAN/PC support | | | | | | | |
| Manager, Quality Assurance | | | | | | | |
| QUALITY ASSURANCE Engineer | | | | | | | |
| **Office** | | | | | | | |
| Office Manager | | | | | | | |
| Receptionist | | | | | | | |
| **Total Salary Expense** | | | | | | | |
| **Benefits @ 25%** | | | | | | | |
| **Bonuses** | | | | | | | |
| **Recruiting fees@25%** | | | | | | | |

## Tech. Budget Worksheet

page 3

| Staffing Outsourced Developmental Costs; | Hourly $ | # Hours | Year 1 1st Qtr | Year 1 2nd Qtr | Year 1 3rd Qtr | Year 1 4th Qtr | Year 2 1st Qtr |
|---|---|---|---|---|---|---|---|
| Project mgr/senior dev | 150-250 | 200 | | | | | |
| Senior developer | 150-200 | 175 | | | | | |
| Database Developer | 125-175 | 150 | | | | | |
| Database admin | 125-175 | 150 | | | | | |
| Developers/programmers | 120-175 | 135 | | | | | |
| Operations staff | 115-135 | 125 | | | | | |
| System admin | 115-150 | 125 | | | | | |
| Firewall admin | 115-150 | 125 | | | | | |
| Networking | 115-150 | 125 | | | | | |
| **Total** | | | | | | | |

(Amounts listed in above worksheet represent only a *possible range* that could be used.)

## Vendor Chart

page 1

| Criteria | Weight | Vendor 1 Score | Vendor 1 Weighted Score | Vendor 2 Score | Vendor 2 Weighted Score | Vendor 2 Score | Vendor 2 Weighted Score |
|---|---|---|---|---|---|---|---|
| | Col A | Col B | A X B | Col C | A X C | Col D | A X D |
| Design | | | | | | | |
| Programming Skills | | | | | | | |
| Maintenance required on system | | | | | | | |
| Project management abilities of vendor | | | | | | | |
| Integration with legacy systems | | | | | | | |
| Performs system functions defined in specifications | | | | | | | |
| Performance related issues: | | | | | | | |
| Time it takes to perform defined functions | | | | | | | |
| Speed at which users receive a response from the system | | | | | | | |
| Communications rates | | | | | | | |
| Data Storage and retrieval | | | | | | | |
| Production and reports | | | | | | | |
| System backups | | | | | | | |
| Other | | | | | | | |
| Other | | | | | | | |

page 2

## Vendor Chart

| Criteria | Weight | Vendor 1 Score | Vendor 1 Weighted Score | Vendor 2 Score | Vendor 2 Weighted Score | Vendor 2 Score | Vendor 2 Weighted Score |
|---|---|---|---|---|---|---|---|
| | Col A | Col B | A X B | Col C | A X C | Col D | A X D |
| Vendor Plan shows deliverable components and a timetable for each delivery | | | | | | | |
| Plan shows cost of each component and conditions under which payments will be made (payment cycle allows time for testing, etc.) | | | | | | | |
| Plan shows testing procedures for acceptance and related payments for accepted components | | | | | | | |
| Plan shows final testing of integrated components in one system | | | | | | | |
| Communications issues—specifically, capacity and reliability (guarantees on uptime and ability to connect to the website | | | | | | | |
| Planning for peak load capacity (X number of simultaneous users) | | | | | | | |
| Compatibility with other systems | | | | | | | |

## Vendor Chart

page 3

| Criteria | Weight | Vendor 1 Score | Vendor 1 Weighted Score | Vendor 2 Score | Vendor 2 Weighted Score | Vendor 2 Score | Vendor 2 Weighted Score |
|---|---|---|---|---|---|---|---|
| | Col A | Col B | A X B | Col C | A X C | Col D | A X D |
| Interaction with other systems (input produced for other systems, such as inventory or financial systems, and output to be accepted from other systems, such as credit card authorization) | | | | | | | |
| Future upgrades | | | | | | | |
| Maintenance issues such as data backups, phone support and onsite support, including response times and the scope of ongoing responsibilities | | | | | | | |
| Other: | | | | | | | |
| | | | | | | | |

# Index

# About the Authors

**Hugo Barreca** holds an M.B.A. from New York University and a J.D. from Fordham University School of Law. He is admitted to the New York, Connecticut and Florida bars. He is a consultant on general management, financial, and legal affairs and has assisted in the formation and organization of several start-up companies. Mr. Barreca resides in the New York area.

**Julia K. O'Neill** earned her degree cum laude at Boston College Law School. She practiced with a firm in Boston for nine years before she and her husband opened their own firm, where she specializes in business, corporate and securities law. Ms. O'Neill resides in the Boston area.

*Your #1 Source for Real World Legal Information...*

# Sphinx® Publishing
### An Imprint of Sourcebooks, Inc.®

- Written by lawyers  • Simple English explanation of the law
  • Forms and instructions included

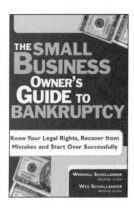

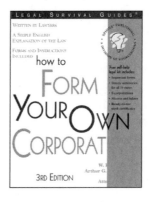

## THE SMALL BUSINESS OWNER'S GUIDE TO BANKRUPTCY

This book gives a general overview of the financial challenges that need to be addressed by the small-business owner. Includes a complete glossary and state-specific homestead and tax exemptions.

240 pages; $21.95;
ISBN 1-57248-219-2

## HOW TO FORM YOUR OWN CORPORATION, 3RD ED.

Contains all the information you need to know to form your own corporation. This book also includes law summaries for all 50 states and the District of Columbia, as well as ready-to-use legal forms.

224 pages; $24.95;
ISBN 1-57248-133-1

*What our customers say about our books:*

"It couldn't be more clear for the layperson." —R.D.

"I want you to know I really appreciate your book. It has saved me a lot of time and money." —L.T.

"Your real estate contracts book has saved me nearly $12,000.00 in closing costs over the past year." —A.B.

"...many of the legal questions that I have had over the years were answered clearly and concisely through your plain English interpretation of the law." —C.E.H.

"If there weren't people out there like you I'd be lost. You have the best books of this type out there." —S.B.

"...your forms and directions are easy to follow." —C.V.M.

*Sphinx Publishing's Legal Survival Guides are directly available from Sourcebooks, Inc., or from your local bookstores.*

*For credit card orders call 1–800–432-7444,*
*write P.O. Box 4410, Naperville, IL 60567-4410, or fax 630-961-2168*
Find more legal information at: **www.SphinxLegal.com**

# Sphinx® Publishing's State Titles
## Up-to-Date for Your State

### California

| | |
|---|---|
| CA Power of Attorney Handbook (2E) | $18.95 |
| How to File for Divorce in CA (3E) | $26.95 |
| How to Make a CA Will | $16.95 |
| How to Probate and Settle an Estate in CA | $26.95 |
| How to Start a Business in CA | $18.95 |
| How to Win in Small Claims Court in CA | $16.95 |
| The Landlord's Legal Guide in CA | $24.95 |

### Florida

| | |
|---|---|
| Florida Power of Attorney Handbook (2E) | $16.95 |
| How to File for Divorce in FL (7E) | $26.95 |
| How to Form a Corporation in FL (5E) | $24.95 |
| How to Form a Limited Liability Company in FL (2E) | $24.95 |
| How to Form a Partnership in FL | $22.95 |
| How to Make a FL Will (6E) | $16.95 |
| How to Modify Your FL Divorce Judgement (4E) | $24.95 |
| How to Probate and Settle an Estate in FL (4E) | $26.95 |
| How to Start a Business in FL (5E) | $16.95 |
| How to Win in Small Claims Court in FL (7E) | $18.95 |
| Land Trusts in Florida (6E) | $29.95 |
| Landlords' Rights and Duties in FL (8E) | $21.95 |

### Georgia

| | |
|---|---|
| How to File for Divorce in GA (4E) | $21.95 |
| How to Make a GA Will (4E) | $21.95 |
| How to Start a Business in GA (2E) | $16.95 |

### Illinois

| | |
|---|---|
| Child Custody, Visitation, and Support in IL | $24.95 |
| How to File for Divorce in IL (3E) | $24.95 |
| How to Make an IL Will (3E) | $16.95 |
| How to Start a Business in IL (2E) | $18.95 |
| The Landlord's Legal Guide in IL | $24.95 |

### Massachusetts

| | |
|---|---|
| How to File for Divorce in MA (3E) | $24.95 |
| How to Form a Corporation in MA | $24.95 |
| How to Make a MA Will (2E) | $16.95 |
| How to Start a Business in MA (2E) | $18.95 |
| The Landlord's Legal Guide in MA | $24.95 |

### Michigan

| | |
|---|---|
| How to File for Divorce in MI (2E) | $21.95 |
| How to Make a MI Will (3E) | $16.95 |
| How to Start a Business in MI (3E) | $18.95 |

*Sphinx Publishing's Legal Survival Guides are directly available from the publisher,
or from your local bookstores.*

Find more legal information at: **www.SphinxLegal.com**

## MINNESOTA

| | |
|---|---|
| How to File for Divorce in MN | $21.95 |
| How to Form a Corporation in MN | $24.95 |
| How to Make a MN Will (2E) | $16.95 |

## NEW JERSEY

| | |
|---|---|
| How to File for Divorce in NJ | $24.95 |

## NEW YORK

| | |
|---|---|
| Child Custody, Visitation and Support in NY | $26.95 |
| How to File for Divorce in NY (2E) | $26.95 |
| How to Form a Corporation in NY (2E) | $24.95 |
| How to Make a NY Will (2E) | $16.95 |
| How to Start a Business in NY (2E) | $18.95 |
| How to Win in Small Claims Court in NY (2E) | $18.95 |
| Landlords' Legal Guide in NY | $24.95 |
| New York Power of Attorney Handbook | $19.95 |
| Tenants' Rights in NY | $21.95 |

## NORTH CAROLINA

| | |
|---|---|
| How to File for Divorce in NC (3E) | $22.95 |
| How to Make a NC Will (3E) | $16.95 |
| How to Start a Business in NC (3E) | $18.95 |
| Landlords' Rights & Duties in NC | $21.95 |

## OHIO

| | |
|---|---|
| How to File for Divorce in OH, 2E | $24.95 |
| How to Form a Corporation in OH | $24.95 |
| How to Make an OH Will | $16.95 |

## PENNSYLVANIA

| | |
|---|---|
| Child Custody, Visitation and Support in PA | $26.95 |
| How to File for Divorce in PA (3E) | $26.95 |
| How to Make a PA Will (2E) | $16.95 |
| How to Start a Business in PA (2E) | $18.95 |
| The Landlord's Legal Guide in PA | $24.95 |

## TEXAS

| | |
|---|---|
| Child Custody, Visitation, and Support in TX | $22.95 |
| How to File for Divorce in TX (3E) | $24.95 |
| How to Form a Corporation in TX (2E) | $24.95 |
| How to Make a TX Will (3E) | $16.95 |
| How to Probate and Settle an Estate in TX (3E) | $26.95 |
| How to Start a Business in TX (3E) | $18.95 |
| How to Win in Small Claims Court in TX (2E) | $16.95 |
| Landlords' Rights and Duties in TX (2E) | $21.95 |

*For credit card orders call 1–800–432-7444,*
*write P.O. Box 4410, Naperville, IL 60567-4410, or fax 630-961-2168*
Find more legal information at: www.SphinxLegal.com

# SPHINX® PUBLISHING'S NATIONAL TITLES
## *Valid in All 50 States*

### LEGAL SURVIVAL IN BUSINESS

| | |
|---|---|
| The Complete Book of Corporate Forms | $24.95 |
| The Entrepreneur's Internet Handbook | $21.95 |
| How to Form a Limited Liability Company | $22.95 |
| Incorporate in Delaware from Any State | $24.95 |
| Incorporate in Nevada from Any State | $24.95 |
| How to Form a Nonprofit Corporation (2E) | $24.95 |
| How to Form Your Own Corporation (3E) | $24.95 |
| How to Form Your Own Partnership (2E) | $24.95 |
| How to Register Your Own Copyright (4E) | $24.95 |
| How to Register Your Own Trademark (3E) | $21.95 |
| Most Valuable Corporate Forms You'll Ever Need (3E) | $21.95 |
| The Small Business Owner's Guide to Bankruptcy | $21.95 |

### LEGAL SURVIVAL IN COURT

| | |
|---|---|
| Crime Victim's Guide to Justice (2E) | $21.95 |
| Grandparents' Rights (3E) | $24.95 |
| Help Your Lawyer Win Your Case (2E) | $14.95 |
| Jurors' Rights (2E) | $12.95 |
| Legal Research Made Easy (3E) | $21.95 |
| Winning Your Personal Injury Claim (2E) | $24.95 |
| Your Rights When You Owe Too Much | $16.95 |

### LEGAL SURVIVAL IN REAL ESTATE

| | |
|---|---|
| Essential Guide to Real Estate Contracts | $18.95 |
| Essential Guide to Real Estate Leases | $18.95 |
| How to Buy a Condominium or Townhome (2E) | $19.95 |

### LEGAL SURVIVAL IN PERSONAL AFFAIRS

| | |
|---|---|
| The 529 College Savings Plan | $16.95 |
| The Complete Legal Guide to Senior Care | $21.95 |
| How to File Your Own Bankruptcy (5E) | $21.95 |
| How to File Your Own Divorce (4E) | $24.95 |
| How to Make Your Own Simple Will (3E) | $18.95 |
| How to Write Your Own Living Will (3E) | $18.95 |
| How to Write Your Own Premarital Agreement (3E) | $24.95 |
| Living Trusts and Other Ways to Avoid Probate (3E) | $24.95 |
| Mastering the MBE | $16.95 |
| Most Valuable Personal Legal Forms You'll Ever Need | $24.95 |
| Neighbor v. Neighbor (2E) | $16.95 |
| The Nanny and Domestic Help Legal Kit | $22.95 |
| The Power of Attorney Handbook (4E) | $19.95 |
| Repair Your Own Credit and Deal with Debt | $18.95 |
| Sexual Harassment: Your Guide to Legal Action | $18.95 |
| The Social Security Benefits Handbook (3E) | $18.95 |
| Social Security Q&A | $12.95 |
| Teen Rights | $22.95 |
| Unmarried Parents' Rights (2E) | $19.95 |
| U.S. Immigration Step By Step | $21.95 |
| U.S.A. Immigration Guide (4E) | $24.95 |
| The Visitation Handbook | $18.95 |
| Win Your Unemployment Compensation Claim (2E) | $21.95 |
| Your Right to Child Custody, Visitation, and Support (2E) | $24.95 |

### LEGAL SURVIVAL IN SPANISH

| | |
|---|---|
| Cómo Hacer su Propio Testamento | $16.95 |
| Cómo Restablecer su propio Crédito y Renegociar sus Deudas | $21.95 |
| Cómo Solicitar su Propio Divorcio | $24.95 |
| Guía de Inmigración a Estados Unidos (3E) | $24.95 |
| Guía de Justicia para Víctimas del Crimen | $21.95 |
| Manual de Beneficios para el Seguro Social | $18.95 |

# SPHINX® PUBLISHING ORDER FORM

<table>
<tr><td>BILL TO:</td><td colspan="2">SHIP TO:</td><td></td></tr>
<tr><td></td><td colspan="3"></td></tr>
<tr><td></td><td colspan="3"></td></tr>
<tr><td>Phone #</td><td>Terms</td><td>F.O.B. Chicago, IL</td><td>Ship Date</td></tr>
</table>

**Charge my:** ☐ VISA  ☐ MasterCard  ☐ American Express  ☐ **Money Order or Personal Check**

| | | | | | | | | | | | | | | | | |
|-|-|-|-|-|-|-|-|-|-|-|-|-|-|-|-|-|

**Credit Card Number**                          **Expiration Date**

| Qty | ISBN | Title | Retail |
|-----|------|-------|--------|
| | | **SPHINX PUBLISHING NATIONAL TITLES** | |
| ___ | 1-57248-148-X | Cómo Hacer su Propio Testamento | $16.95 |
| ___ | 1-57248-226-5 | Cómo Restablecer su propio Crédito y Renegociar sus Deudas | $21.95 |
| ___ | 1-57248-147-1 | Cómo Solicitar su Propio Divorcio | $24.95 |
| ___ | 1-57248-238-9 | The 529 College Savings Plan | $16.95 |
| ___ | 1-57248-166-8 | The Complete Book of Corporate Forms | $24.95 |
| ___ | 1-57248-229-X | The Complete Legal Guide to Senior Care | $21.95 |
| ___ | 1-57248-163-3 | Crime Victim's Guide to Justice (2E) | $21.95 |
| ___ | 1-57248-251-6 | The Entrepreneur's Internet Handbook | $21.95 |
| ___ | 1-57248-159-5 | Essential Guide to Real Estate Contracts | $18.95 |
| ___ | 1-57248-160-9 | Essential Guide to Real Estate Leases | $18.95 |
| ___ | 1-57248-139-0 | Grandparents' Rights (3E) | $24.95 |
| ___ | 1-57248-188-9 | Guia de Inmigración a Estados Unidos (3E) | $24.95 |
| ___ | 1-57248-187-0 | Guia de Justicia para Victimas del Crimen | $21.95 |
| ___ | 1-57248-103-X | Help Your Lawyer Win Your Case (2E) | $14.95 |
| ___ | 1-57248-164-1 | How to Buy a Condominium or Townhome (2E) | $19.95 |
| ___ | 1-57248-191-9 | How to File Your Own Bankruptcy (5E) | $21.95 |
| ___ | 1-57248-132-3 | How to File Your Own Divorce (4E) | $24.95 |
| ___ | 1-57248-083-1 | How to Form a Limited Liability Company | $22.95 |
| ___ | 1-57248-231-1 | How to Form a Nonprofit Corporation (2E) | $24.95 |
| ___ | 1-57248-133-1 | How to Form Your Own Corporation (3E) | $24.95 |
| ___ | 1-57248-224-9 | How to Form Your Own Partnership (2E) | $24.95 |
| ___ | 1-57248-232-X | How to Make Your Own Simple Will (3E) | $18.95 |
| ___ | 1-57248-200-1 | How to Register Your Own Copyright (4E) | $24.95 |
| ___ | 1-57248-104-8 | How to Register Your Own Trademark (3E) | $21.95 |
| ___ | 1-57248-233-8 | How to Write Your Own Living Will (3E) | $18.95 |
| ___ | 1-57248-156-0 | How to Write Your Own Premarital Agreement (3E) | $24.95 |
| ___ | 1-57248-230-3 | Incorporate in Delaware from Any State | $24.95 |
| ___ | 1-57248-158-7 | Incorporate in Nevada from Any State | $24.95 |
| ___ | 1-57071-333-2 | Jurors' Rights (2E) | $12.95 |
| ___ | 1-57248-223-0 | Legal Research Made Easy (3E) | $21.95 |
| ___ | 1-57248-165-X | Living Trusts and Other Ways to Avoid Probate (3E) | $24.95 |
| ___ | 1-57248-186-2 | Manual de Beneficios para el Seguro Social | $18.95 |
| ___ | 1-57248-220-6 | Mastering the MBE | $16.95 |
| ___ | 1-57248-167-6 | Most Valuable Bus. Legal Forms You'll Ever Need (3E) | $21.95 |

| Qty | ISBN | Title | Retail |
|-----|------|-------|--------|
| ___ | 1-57248-130-7 | Most Valuable Personal Legal Forms You'll Ever Need | $24.95 |
| ___ | 1-57248-098-X | The Nanny and Domestic Help Legal Kit | $22.95 |
| ___ | 1-57248-089-0 | Neighbor v. Neighbor (2E) | $16.95 |
| ___ | 1-57248-169-2 | The Power of Attorney Handbook (4E) | $19.95 |
| ___ | 1-57248-149-8 | Repair Your Own Credit and Deal with Debt | $18.95 |
| ___ | 1-57248-217-6 | Sexual Harassment: Your Guide to Legal Action | $18.95 |
| ___ | 1-57248-219-2 | The Small Business Owner's Guide to Bankruptcy | $21.95 |
| ___ | 1-57248-168-4 | The Social Security Benefits Handbook (3E) | $18.95 |
| ___ | 1-57248-216-8 | Social Security Q&A | $12.95 |
| ___ | 1-57248-221-4 | Teen Rights | $22.95 |
| ___ | 1-57248-236-2 | Unmarried Parents' Rights (2E) | $19.95 |
| ___ | 1-57248-218-4 | U.S. Immigration Step-by-Step | $21.95 |
| ___ | 1-57248-161-7 | U.S.A. Immigration Guide (4E) | $24.95 |
| ___ | 1-57248-192-7 | The Visitation Handbook | $18.95 |
| ___ | 1-57248-225-7 | Win Your Unemployment Compensation Claim (2E) | $21.95 |
| ___ | 1-57248-138-2 | Winning Your Personal Injury Claim (2E) | $24.95 |
| ___ | 1-57248-162-5 | Your Right to Child Custody, Visitation, and Support (2E) | $24.95 |
| ___ | 1-57248-157-9 | Your Rights When You Owe Too Much | $16.95 |
| | | **CALIFORNIA TITLES** | |
| ___ | 1-57248-150-1 | CA Power of Attorney Handbook (2E) | $18.95 |
| ___ | 1-57248-151-X | How to File for Divorce in CA (3E) | $26.95 |
| ___ | 1-57071-356-1 | How to Make a CA Will | $16.95 |
| ___ | 1-57248-145-5 | How to Probate and Settle and Estate in CA | $26.95 |
| ___ | 1-57248-146-3 | How to Start a Business in CA | $18.95 |
| ___ | 1-57248-194-3 | How to Win in Small Claims Court in CA (2E) | $18.95 |
| ___ | 1-57248-196-X | The Landlord's Legal Guide in CA | $24.95 |
| | | **FLORIDA TITLES** | |
| ___ | 1-57071-363-4 | Florida Power of Attorney Handbook (2E) | $16.95 |
| ___ | 1-57248-176-5 | How to File for Divorce in FL (7E) | $26.95 |
| ___ | 1-57248-177-3 | How to Form a Corporation in FL (5E) | $24.95 |
| ___ | 1-57248-203-6 | How to Form a Limited Liability Co. in FL (2E) | $24.95 |
| ___ | 1-57071-401-0 | How to Form a Partnership in FL | $22.95 |

*Form Continued on Following Page*                          **Subtotal** _____

| Qty | ISBN | Title | Retail |
|-----|------|-------|--------|
| | | **FLORIDA TITLES (CONT'D)** | |
| _____ | 1-57248-113-7 | How to Make a FL Will (6E) | $16.95 |
| _____ | 1-57248-088-2 | How to Modify Your FL Divorce Judgment (4E) | $24.95 |
| _____ | 1-57248-144-7 | How to Probate and Settle an Estate in FL (4E) | $26.95 |
| _____ | 1-57248-081-5 | How to Start a Business in FL (5E) | $16.95 |
| _____ | 1-57248-204-4 | How to Win in Small Claims Court in FL (7E) | $18.95 |
| _____ | 1-57248-202-8 | Land Trusts in Florida (6E) | $29.95 |
| _____ | 1-57248-123-4 | Landlords' Rights and Duties in FL (8E) | $21.95 |
| | | **GEORGIA TITLES** | |
| _____ | 1-57248-137-4 | How to File for Divorce in GA (4E) | $21.95 |
| _____ | 1-57248-180-3 | How to Make a GA Will (4E) | $21.95 |
| _____ | 1-57248-140-4 | How to Start Business in GA (2E) | $16.95 |
| | | **ILLINOIS TITLES** | |
| _____ | 1-57248-244-3 | Child Custody, Visitation, and Support in IL | $24.95 |
| _____ | 1-57248-206-0 | How to File for Divorce in IL (3E) | $24.95 |
| _____ | 1-57248-170-6 | How to Make an IL Will (3E) | $16.95 |
| _____ | 1-57248-247-8 | How to Start a Business in IL (3E) | $21.95 |
| _____ | 1-57248-252-4 | The Landlord's Legal Guide in IL | $24.95 |
| | | **MASSACHUSETTS TITLES** | |
| _____ | 1-57248-128-5 | How to File for Divorce in MA (3E) | $24.95 |
| _____ | 1-57248-115-3 | How to Form a Corporation in MA | $24.95 |
| _____ | 1-57248-108-0 | How to Make a MA Will (2E) | $16.95 |
| _____ | 1-57248-106-4 | How to Start a Business in MA (2E) | $18.95 |
| _____ | 1-57248-209-5 | The Landlord's Legal Guide in MA | $24.95 |
| | | **MICHIGAN TITLES** | |
| _____ | 1-57248-215-X | How to File for Divorce in MI (3E) | $24.95 |
| _____ | 1-57248-182-X | How to Make a MI Will (3E) | $16.95 |
| _____ | 1-57248-183-8 | How to Start a Business in MI (3E) | $18.95 |
| | | **MINNESOTA TITLES** | |
| _____ | 1-57248-142-0 | How to File for Divorce in MN | $21.95 |
| _____ | 1-57248-179-X | How to Form a Corporation in MN | $24.95 |
| _____ | 1-57248-178-1 | How to Make a MN Will (2E) | $16.95 |
| | | **NEW JERSEY TITLES** | |
| _____ | 1-57248-239-7 | How to File for Divorce in NJ | $24.95 |
| | | **NEW YORK TITLES** | |
| _____ | 1-57248-193-5 | Child Custody, Visitation and Support in NY | $26.95 |
| _____ | 1-57248-141-2 | How to File for Divorce in NY (2E) | $26.95 |
| _____ | 1-57248-249-4 | How to Form a Corporation in NY (2EO) | $24.95 |
| _____ | 1-57248-095-5 | How to Make a NY Will (2E) | $16.95 |
| _____ | 1-57248-199-4 | How to Start a Business in NY (2E) | $18.95 |
| _____ | 1-57248-198-6 | How to Win in Small Claims Court in NY (2E) | $18.95 |
| _____ | 1-57248-197-8 | Landlords' Legal Guide in NY | $24.95 |
| _____ | 1-57071-188-7 | New York Power of Attorney Handbook | $19.95 |
| _____ | 1-57248-122-6 | Tenants' Rights in New York | $21.95 |
| | | **NORTH CAROLINA TITLES** | |
| _____ | 1-57248-185-4 | How to File for Divorce in NC (3E) | $22.95 |
| _____ | 1-57248-129-3 | How to Make a NC Will (3E) | $16.95 |
| _____ | 1-57248-184-6 | How to Start a Business in NC (3E) | $18.95 |
| _____ | 1-57248-091-2 | Landlords' Rights & Duties in NC | $21.95 |
| | | **OHIO TITLES** | |
| _____ | 1-57248-190-0 | How to File for Divorce in OH (2E) | $24.95 |
| _____ | 1-57248-174-9 | How to Form a Corporation in OH | $24.95 |
| _____ | 1-57248-173-0 | How to Make an OH Will | $16.95 |
| | | **PENNSYLVANIA TITLES** | |
| _____ | 1-57248-242-7 | Child Custody, Visitation and Support in PA | $26.95 |
| _____ | 1-57248-211-7 | How to File for Divorce in PA (3E) | $26.95 |
| _____ | 1-57248-094-7 | How to Make a PA Will (2E) | $16.95 |
| _____ | 1-57248-112-9 | How to Start a Business in PA (2E) | $18.95 |
| _____ | 1-57248-245-1 | The Landlord's Legal Guide in PA | $24.95 |
| | | **TEXAS TITLES** | |
| _____ | 1-57248-171-4 | Child Custody, Visitation, and Support in TX | $22.95 |
| _____ | 1-57248-172-2 | How to File for Divorce in TX (3E) | $24.95 |
| _____ | 1-57248-114-5 | How to Form a Corporation in TX (2E) | $24.95 |
| _____ | 1-57248-255-9 | How to Make a TX Will (3E) | $16.95 |
| _____ | 1-57248-214-1 | How to Probate and Settle an Estate in TX (3E) | $26.95 |
| _____ | 1-57248-228-1 | How to Start a Business in TX (3E) | $18.95 |
| _____ | 1-57248-111-0 | How to Win in Small Claims Court in TX (2E) | $16.95 |
| _____ | 1-57248-110-2 | Landlords' Rights and Duties in TX (2E) | $21.95 |

**SUBTOTAL THIS PAGE** _____

**SUBTOTAL PREVIOUS PAGE** _____

Shipping— $5.00 for 1st book, $1.00 each additional _____

Illinois residents add 6.75% sales tax _____

Connecticut residents add 6.00% sales tax _____

**TOTAL** _____